THE
SCARLET LETTER

AN ADAPTED CLASSIC

THE
SCARLET LETTER

NATHANIEL HAWTHORNE

GLOBE FEARON
Pearson Learning Group

Cover design: Marek Antoniak
Cover illustration: Richard Martin
Text illustrations: Ken Hamilton

ISBN 0-8359-0262-5
Printed in the United States of America

13 14 15 16 17 18   05 04 03 02

1-800-321-3106
www.pearsonlearning.com

About the Author

Born in Salem, Massachusetts, in 1804, Nathaniel Hawthorne is one of America's major authors. During his youth, Hawthorne sharpened his writing talent by reading widely and studying the history of his family, the Hathornes. He changed the spelling of his name to Hawthorne after the publication of his first stories.

In 1825, Hawthorne was graduated from Bowdoin College in Maine. The friendship of three of his classmates there had a lasting influence on his life. Horatio Bridge, who encouraged Hawthorne to overcome his timidity by involving himself in campus life, later helped pay for the publication of his collected stories, *Twice-Told Tales*. Franklin Pierce, the 14th United States President, appointed his old friend to an important political post in the British consulate. A third classmate, Henry Wadsworth Longfellow, helped draw critics' attention to Hawthorne's work, assuring its acceptance by readers of the time.

Hawthorne could not earn an adequate living from his writing. To support himself, he took jobs in public services. He was a customs agent in Boston when he learned about a woman who was once forced to wear a scarlet letter *A* as punishment for adultery. The result of his interest in this unusual incident was his most famous work, *The Scarlet Letter*, published in 1850.

This novel, and many of Hawthorne's works, including *The House of Seven Gables*, "The Minister's Black Veil," and "Young Goodman Brown," emphasize themes of inner suffering. The darker side of human nature haunts his characters and drives them to often desperate acts. Hawthorne's fiction provides the reader with a valuable analysis of the human struggle between good and evil. At the time of his death in 1864, Nathaniel Hawthorne was already considered a great writer and had gained international fame.

Adapter's Note

This adaptation follows the original as faithfully as possible. To make the story more understandable to the modern reader, some of the vocabulary has been simplified.

Preface

Nathaniel Hawthorne spent many years writing short fiction before the publication of *The Scarlet Letter*. During the years the author spent refining his talent, he was also developing a keen interest in the past and studying the history of his own family. The period which interested Hawthorne most was the 17th century, when the Massachusetts Colony was a lonely outpost in the New World. Life for the colonists demanded hard work and constant caution against the threats of wild animals, Indian attacks, disease, and hunger.

In addition to these threats, many people of the time feared individuals whom they considered witches. By 1692 in Massachusetts Colony, interest in witchcraft had reached such intensity that more than 100 people were charged with casting spells and practicing magic. The hysteria in New England resulted in a long series of trials, imprisonments, and cruel deaths.

Both religious leaders and government officials expected complete obedience from the new citizens of Massachusetts. Their demands were based on a very strict moral code. People who defied the moral code faced harsh penalties. Adultery, which is the subject of *The Scarlet Letter,* was often punished in front of the entire community. Great wooden platforms provided a stage for public whippings and humiliation. Facing such harsh penalties, the accused person was constantly reminded of the wrongdoing.

In *The Scarlet Letter,* Hawthorne narrates the effects of a single wrongful act upon the lives of four people. Hester Prynne, the main character, willingly accepts her public punishment for the crime of adultery. Using her skill as a seamstress, she embroiders a fancy letter *A*, which she wears on her clothing for all to see.

Hester is not alone in facing the effects of her crime. Her illegitimate daughter Pearl, isolated because of the disapproval of the townspeople, develops into a stubborn, unmanageable child. Hester's minister, the Reverend Arthur Dimmesdale, and his physician, Roger Chillingsworth, are also caught up in Hester's crime. Through the interactions of these four characters, the plot of *The Scarlet Letter* unfolds.

Their suffering represents Hawthorne's belief that people who hide their wrongdoings do not escape the results of sin. Although Hester finds a useful place for herself as nurse and seamstress in the community, she never escapes the unhappiness caused by her long-kept secret or the effects of her crime. Even in death, Hester lies beneath a tombstone inscribed with an *A*, a reminder to all of her weakness.

> Mary Ellen Snodgrass
> former English Department Chairperson
> Hickory High School
> Hickory, North Carolina

CONTENTS

1 *The Prison-Door*

A throng of bearded men, in sad-colored garments, and gray, steeple-crowned hats, intermixed with women, some wearing hoods and others bareheaded, was assembled in front of a wooden building, the door of which was heavily timbered with oak, and studded with iron spikes.

The founders of a new colony, whatever Utopia[1] of human virtue and happiness they might originally project, have always recognized it among their earliest practical necessities to allot a portion of the virgin soil as a cemetery, and another portion as the site of a prison. In accordance with this rule, it may safely be taken for granted that the forefathers of Boston had built the first prison-house somewhere in the vicinity of Cornhill, almost as seasonably as they marked out the first burial ground, on Isaac Johnson's lot, and round about his grave, which subsequently became the nucleus of all the congregated sepulchres[2] in the old churchyard of King's Chapel. Certain it is, that, some fifteen or twenty years after the settlement of the town, the wooden jail was already marked with weatherstains and other signs of age, which gave a yet darker aspect to its beetle-browed and gloomy front. The rust on the ponderous iron-work of its oaken door looked more antique

[1] Utopia: an ideal place, described in a book by Sir Thomas More

[2] sepulchres: tombs

than anything else in the New World. Like all that pertains to crime, it seemed never to have known a youthful era. Before this ugly edifice, and between it and the wheel-track of the street, was a grass-plot, much overgrown with burdock, pigweed, apple peru,[3] and such unsightly vegetation, which evidently found something congenial in the soil that had so early borne the black flower of civilized society, a prison. But, on one side of the portal, and rooted almost at the threshold, was a wild rosebush, covered, in this month of June, with its delicate gems, which might be imagined to offer their fragrance and fragile beauty to the prisoner as he went in, and to the condemned criminal as he came forth to his doom, in token that the deep heart of Nature could pity and be kind to him.

This rosebush, by a strange chance, has been kept alive in history; but whether it had merely survived out of the stern old wilderness, so long after the fall of the gigantic pines and oaks that originally overshadowed it—or whether, as there is fair authority for believing, it had sprung up under the footsteps of the sainted Anne Hutchinson,[4] as she entered the prison-door,—we shall not determine. Finding it so directly on the threshold of our narrative, which is now about to issue from that unlucky portal, we could hardly do otherwise than pluck one of its flowers, and present it to the reader. It may serve, let us hope, to stand for some sweet moral blossom, that may be found along the track, or relieve the darkening close of a tale of human weakness and sorrow.

[3] burdock, pigweed, apple peru: ugly weeds

[4] Anne Hutchinson: a religious leader (1591–1643), banished from the Massachusetts Colony

there was very much the same sober behavior on the part of the spectators; as befitted a people amongst whom religion and law were almost identical, and in whose character both were so thoroughly combined, that the mildest and the severest acts of public discipline were alike made venerable and awful.[2] Slight, indeed, and cold was the sympathy that a sinner might look for from such bystanders, at the scaffold. On the other hand, a penalty, which, in our days, would infer a degree of mocking infamy and ridicule, might then be invested with almost as stern a dignity as the punishment of death itself.

It was a circumstance to be noted, on the summer morning when our story begins its course, that the women, of whom there were several in the crowd, appeared to take a peculiar interest in whatever penal infliction might be expected to ensue. The age had not so much refinement, that any sense of impropriety restrained the wearers of petticoat and hoop skirt from stepping forth into the public ways, and wedging their not unsubstantial persons, if occasion were, into the throng nearest to the scaffold at an execution. Morally, as well as materially, there was a coarser fibre in those wives and maidens of old English birth and breeding, than in their fair descendants, separated from them by a series of six or seven generations; for, throughout that chain of ancestry, every successive mother has transmitted to her child a fainter bloom, a more delicate and briefer beauty, and a slighter physical frame, if not a character of less force and solidity, than her own. The women who were now standing about the prison-door stood within less than half a century of the period when the man-like Elizabeth had been the not altogether unsuitable representative of the sex. They were her countrywomen; and the beef and ale of their native land, with a moral diet not a whit more refined, entered largely into

---

[2] venerable and awful: impressive and awe-inspiring

their composition. The bright morning sun, therefore, shone on broad shoulders and well-developed bodies, and on round and ruddy cheeks, that had ripened in the far-off island, and had hardly yet grown paler or thinner in the atmosphere of New England. There was, moreover, a boldness and richness of speech among these matrons, as most of them seemed to be, that would startle us at the present day, whether in respect to its purport or its volume of tone.

"Goodwives," said a hard-featured dame of fifty, "I'll tell ye a piece of my mind. It would be greatly for the public behoof,[3] if we women, being of mature age and church-members in good repute, should have the handling of such malefactresses[4] as this Hester Prynne. What think ye, gossips?[5] If the hussy stood up for judgment before us five, that are now here in a knot together, would she come off with such a sentence as the worshipful magistrates have awarded? I think not!"

"People say," said another, "that the Reverend Master Dimmesdale, her godly pastor, takes it very grievously to heart that such a scandal should have come upon his congregation."

"The magistrates are God-fearing gentlemen, but merciful overmuch,—that is the truth," added a third middle-aged matron. "At the very least, they should have put the brand of a hot iron on Hester Prynne's forehead. Madame Hester would have winced at that, I warrant me. But she,—the haughty flirt,—little will she care what they put upon the bodice of her gown! Why, look you, she may cover it with a brooch, or such like heathenish adornment, and so walk the streets as brave as ever!"

"Ah, but," interposed, softly, a young wife, holding

---

[3] for the public behoof: in the public interest

[4] malefactresses: evil-doing women

[5] gossips: friends

a child by the hand, "let her cover the mark as she will, the pang of it will always be in her heart."

"What do we talk of marks and brands, whether on her gown, or the flesh of her forehead?" cried another female, the ugliest as well as the most pitiless of these self-appointed judges. "This woman has brought shame upon us all, and ought to die. Is there not law for it? Truly, there is, both in the Scripture and the statute-book. Then let the magistrates, who have made it of no effect, thank themselves if their own wives and daughters go astray!"

"Mercy on us, goodwife," exclaimed a man in the crowd, "is there no virtue in woman, save what springs from a wholesome fear of the gallows? That is the hardest word yet! Hush now, gossips! for the lock is turning in the prison-door, and here comes Mistress Prynne herself."

The door of the jail being flung open from within, there appeared, in the first place, like a black shadow emerging into sunshine, the grim and grisly presence of the town-beadle,[6] with his sword by his side, and his staff of office in his hand. This person represented in his aspect the whole dismal severity of the Puritanic code of law, which it was his business to administer in its final and closest application to the offender. Stretching forth the official staff in his left hand, he laid his right upon the shoulder of a young woman, whom he thus drew forward; until, on the threshold of the prison-door, she repelled him, by an action marked with natural dignity and force of character, and stepped into the open air, as if by her own free will. She bore in her arms a child, a baby of some three months old, who winked and turned aside its little face from the too vivid light of day; because its existence had made it acquainted only with the gray twilight of a dungeon, or other dark apartment[7] of the prison.

6 beadle: a minor official of the law court

7 apartment: compartment

When the young woman—the mother of this child—stood fully revealed before the crowd, it seemed to be her first impulse to clasp the infant closely to her bosom; not so much by an impulse of motherly affection, as that she might thereby conceal a certain token, which was wrought or fastened into her dress. In a moment, however, wisely judging that one token of her shame would but poorly serve to hide another, she took the baby on her arm, and, with a burning blush, and yet a haughty smile, and a glance that would not be abashed, looked around at her townspeople and neighbors. On the breast of her gown, in fine red cloth, surrounded with an elaborate embroidery and fantastic flourishes of gold-thread, appeared the letter A. It was so artistically done, and with so much fertility and gorgeous luxuriance of fancy, that it had all the effect of a last and fitting decoration to the apparel which she wore; and which was of a splendor in accordance with the taste of the age, but greatly beyond what was allowed by the strict rules of the colony.

The young woman was tall, with a figure of perfect elegance on a large scale. She had dark and abundant hair, so glossy that it threw off the sunshine with a gleam, and a face which, besides being beautiful from regularity of feature and richness of complexion, had the impressiveness belonging to a marked brow and deep black eyes. She was lady-like, too, after the manner of the feminine gentility of those days; characterized by a certain state and dignity, rather than by the delicate, fading and indescribable grace, which is now recognized as its indication. And never had Hester Prynne appeared more ladylike, than as she issued from the prison. Those who had before known her, and had expected to behold her dimmed and obscured by a disastrous cloud, were astonished, to perceive how her beauty shone out, and made a halo of the misfortune and shame in which she was enveloped. It may be true,

that, to a sensitive observer, there was something exquis-
itely painful in it. Her dress, which, indeed, she had carefully wrought for the occasion, in prison, and had modelled
much after her own fancy, seemed to express the attitude
of her spirit, the desperate recklessness of her mood, by
its wild and picturesque peculiarity. But the point which
drew all eyes, and, as it were, transfigured the wearer,—
so that both men and women, who had been familiarly
acquainted with Hester Prynne, now felt as if they beheld
her for the first time,—was that SCARLET LETTER, so fantastically embroidered and illuminated upon her bosom. It
had the effect of a spell, taking her out of the ordinary
relations with humanity, and enclosing her in a sphere by
herself.

"She hath good skill at her needle, that's certain,"
remarked one of her female spectators; "but did ever a
woman, before this brazen hussy, contrive such a way of
showing it! Why, gossips, what is it but to laugh in the
faces of our godly magistrates, and make a pride out of
what they, worthy gentlemen, meant for a punishment?"

"It were well," muttered the most iron-faced of the old
dames, "if we stripped Madam Hester's rich gown off her
dainty shoulders; and as for the red letter, which she hath
stitched so curiously, I'll bestow a rag of mine own rheu-
matic flannel, to make a fitter one!"

"Oh, peace, neighbor, peace!" whispered their youngest companion; "do not let her hear you! Not a stitch in
that embroidered letter, but she has felt in her heart."

The grim beadle now made a gesture with his staff.

"Make way, good people, make way, in the King's
name!" cried he. "Open a passage; and, I promise ye,
Mistress Prynne shall be set where man, woman, and child
may have a fair sight of her brave[8] apparel, from this time
till an hour past noontime. A blessing on the righteous

[8] brave: bright, colorful

Colony of the Massachusetts, where iniquity is dragged out into the sunshine! Come along, Madam Hester, and show your scarlet letter in the market place!"

A lane was forthwith opened through the crowd of spectators. Preceded by the beadle, and attended by an irregular procession of stern-browed men and unkindly visaged women, Hester Prynne set forth towards the place appointed for her punishment. A crowd of eager and curious schoolboys, understanding little of the matter in hand, except that it gave them a half-holiday, ran before her progress, turning their heads continually to stare into her face, and at the winking baby in her arms, and at the shameful letter on her breast. It was no great distance, in those days, from the prison-door to the market place. Measured by the prisoner's experience, however, it might be reckoned a journey of some length; for, haughty as her demeanor was, she underwent an agony from every footstep of those that thronged to see her, as if her heart had been flung into the street for them all to trample upon. In our nature, however, there is a provision, both marvellous and merciful, that the sufferer should never know the intensity of what he endures by its present torture, but chiefly by the pang that rankles after it. With almost a serene manner, therefore, Hester Prynne passed through this portion of her ordeal, and came to a sort of scaffold, at the western extremity of the market place. It stood nearly beneath the eaves of Boston's earliest church, and appeared to be a fixture there.

In fact, this scaffold constituted a portion of a penal machine, which now, for two or three generations past, has been merely historical and traditionary among us, but was held, in the old time, to be as effectual an agent, in promoting good citizenship, as ever was the guillotine among the terrorists of France. It was, in short, the platform of the pillory; and above it rose the framework of that instrument of discipline, so fashioned as to confine the human head in its tight grasp, thus holding it up to the public gaze. The very ideal of ignominy was embodied in this contrivance of wood and iron. There can be no outrage, methinks, against our common nature,—whatever be the delinquencies of the individual,—no outrage more flagrant than to forbid the culprit to hide his face for shame; as it was the essence of this punishment to do. In Hester Prynne's instance, however, as not infrequently in other cases, her sentence bore, that she should stand a certain time upon the platform, but without undergoing that gripe about the neck and confinement of the head, the proneness to which was the most devilish characteristic of this ugly engine. Knowing well her part, she mounted a flight of wooden steps, and was thus displayed to the surrounding multitude, at about the height of a man's shoulders above the street.

Had there been a Papist[9] among the crowd of Puritans, he might have seen in this beautiful woman, so pictur- esque in her attire and mien, and with the infant at her bosom, an object to remind him of the image of Divine Maternity, which so many illustrious painters have vied with one another to represent; something which should remind him, indeed, but only by contrast, of that sacred image of sinless motherhood, whose infant was to redeem the world.

The scene was not without a mixture of awe, such as must always invest the spectacle of guilt and shame in a fellow-creature, before society shall have grown corrupt enough to smile, instead of shuddering, at it. The witnesses of Hester Prynne's disgrace had not yet passed beyond their simplicity. They were stern enough to look upon her death, had that been the sentence, without a murmur at its severity, but had none of the heartlessness of another

9 Papist: a Roman Catholic; generally used in an unfriendly sense

social state, which would find only a theme for jest in an exhibition like the present. Even had there been a disposition to turn the matter into ridicule, it must have been repressed and overpowered by the solemn presence of men no less dignified than the Governor, and several of his counsellors; a judge, a general, and the ministers of the town; all of whom sat or stood in a balcony of the meeting house, looking down upon the platform. When such personages could be a part of the spectacle, without risking the majesty or reverence of rank or office, it was safely to be inferred that the infliction of a legal sentence would have an earnest and effectual meaning. Accordingly, the crowd was somber and grave. The unhappy culprit sustained herself as best a woman might, under the heavy weight of a thousand unrelenting eyes, all fastened upon her, and concentrated at her bosom. It was almost intolerable. Of an impulsive nature, she had fortified herself to encounter the stings and venomous stabs of public insult, but there was a quality so much more terrible in the solemn mood of the popular mind, that she longed rather to behold all those rigid countenances contorted with scornful merriment, and herself the object. Had a roar of laughter burst from the multitude,—Hester Prynne might have repaid them all with a bitter and disdainful smile. But, under the leaden infliction which it was her doom to endure, she felt, at moments, as if she must shriek out with all the power of her lungs, and cast herself from the scaffold down upon the ground, or else go mad.

Yet there were intervals when the whole scene, in which she was the most conspicuous object, seemed to vanish from her eyes, or, at least, glimmered indistinctly before them, like a mass of imperfectly shaped and spectral images. Memories the most trifling and immaterial, scenes of infancy and school-days, sports, childish quarrels, and the little domestic traits of her maiden years, came swarming back upon her, mixed with recollections of whatever was gravest in her subsequent life; one picture precisely as vivid as another; as if all were of similar importance, or all alike a play. Possibly, it was an instinctive device of her spirit, to relieve itself, by the exhibition of these confusing forms, from the cruel weight and hardness of the reality.

Be that as it might, the scaffold of the pillory was a point of view that revealed to Hester Prynne the entire track along which she had been treading since her happy infancy. Standing on that miserable height, she saw again her native village, in Old England, and her paternal home; a decayed house of gray stone, with a poverty-stricken aspect, but retaining a half-obliterated shield of arms over the portal, in sign of antique gentility. She saw her father's face, with its bald brow, and reverend white beard, that flowed over the old-fashioned Elizabethan ruff;[10] her mother's too, with the look of heedful and anxious love which it always wore in her remembrance, and which, even since her death, had so often laid the obstacle of a gentle remonstrance in her daughter's pathway. She saw her own face, glowing with girlish beauty, and illuminating all the interior of the dusky mirror in which she had been wont to gaze at it. There she beheld another countenance, of a man well stricken in years, a pale, thin, scholar-like visage, with eyes dim and bleared by the lamplight that had served them to pore over many heavy books. Yet those same bleared eyes had a strange, penetrating power, when it was their owner's purpose to read the human soul. This figure of the study and the cloister,[11] as Hester Prynne's womanly fancy recalled, was slightly deformed, with the left shoulder a trifle higher than the right. Next rose before her, in memory's picture-gallery, the intricate and narrow thoroughfares, the tall, gray houses, the huge cathedrals, and

[10] ruff: a round, pleated collar worn by both men and women in the 16th and 17th centuries

[11] cloister: an arched walkway within a college or church building

the public buildings, ancient in date and quaint in archi-
tecture, of a Continental city; where a new life had awaited
her, still in connection with the misshapen scholar; a new
life, but feeding itself on time-worn materials, like a tuft
of green moss on a crumbling wall. Lastly, in lieu of these
shifting scenes, came back the rude market place of the
Puritan settlement, with all the townspeople assembled
and levelling their stern gaze at Hester Prynne,—yes, at
herself,—who stood on the scaffold of the pillory, an infant
on her arm, and the letter A, in scarlet, embroidered with
gold-thread, upon her bosom!

Could it be true? She clutched the child so fiercely to
her breast, that it sent forth a cry; she turned her eyes
downward at the scarlet letter, and even touched it with
her finger, to assure herself that the infant and the shame
were real. Yes!—these were *her* realities,—all else had vanished!

③ *The Recognition*

From this deep awareness of being the object of severe and universal observation, the wearer of the scarlet letter was at length relieved, by noticing, on the outskirts of the crowd, a figure which irresistibly took possession of her thoughts. An Indian, in his native garb, was standing there; but red men were not so infrequent visitors of the English settlements, that one of them would have attracted any notice from Hester Prynne at such a time; much less would he have excluded all other objects and ideals from her mind. By the Indian's side, and evidently his companion, stood a white man, clad in a strange mixture of civilized and savage costume.

He was small in stature, with a furrowed visage, which, as yet, could hardly be termed aged. There was a remarkable intelligence in his features, as of a person who had so cultivated his mental part that it could not fail to mould the physical to itself, and so become manifest by unmistakable tokens. Although, by a seemingly careless arrangement of his mixed garb, he had endeavored to conceal or lessen the peculiarity, it was sufficiently clear to Hester Prynne that one of this man's shoulders rose higher than the other. Again, at the first instant of perceiving that thin face, and the slight deformity of the figure, she pressed her infant to her bosom with such force that the poor babe uttered another cry of pain. But the mother did not seem to hear it.

At his arrival in the market place, and some time before she saw him, the stranger had bent his eyes on Hester Prynne. It was carelessly, at first, like a man chiefly accustomed to look inward, and to whom outside matters are of little value and import, unless they bear relation to something inside his mind. Very soon, however, his look became keen and penetrative. A writhing horror twisted itself across his features, like a snake gliding swiftly over them, and making one little pause, with all its wreathed intervolutions in open sight. His face darkened with some powerful emotion, which, nevertheless, he so instantaneously controlled by an effort of his will, that, save at a single moment, its expression might have passed for calmness. After a brief space, the convulsion grew almost im-

perceptible, and finally subsided. When he found the eyes of Hester Prynne fastened on his own, and saw that she recognized him, he slowly and calmly raised his finger, made a gesture with it in the air, and laid it on his lips.

Then, touching the shoulder of a townsman who stood next to him, he addressed him, in a courteous manner.

"I pray you, good Sir," said he, "who is this woman?— and wherefore is she here set up to public shame?"

"You must be a stranger in this region, friend," answered the townsman, looking curiously at the questioner

and his savage companion, "else you would surely have heard of Miss Hester Prynne, and her evil doings. She hath raised a great scandal, I promise you, in godly Master Dimmesdale's church."

"Yes," replied the other. "I am a stranger, and have been a wanderer, sorely against my will. I have met with grievous mishaps by sea and land, and have been long held in bonds among the heathen-folk, to the southward; and am now brought hither by this Indian to be redeemed out of my captivity. Will it please you, therefore, to tell me of Hester Prynne's—have I her name rightly?—of this woman's offences, and what has brought her to stand on yonder scaffold?"

"Truly, friend; and methinks it must gladden your heart, after your troubles and sojourn[1] in the wilderness," said the townsman, "to find yourself, at length, in a land where iniquity is searched out, and punished in the sight of rulers and people, as here in our godly New England. Yonder woman, Sir, you must know, was the wife of a certain learned man, English by birth, but who had long dwelt in Amsterdam, whence, some good time ago, he was minded to cross over and cast in his lot with us of the Massachusetts. To this purpose, he sent his wife before him, remaining himself to look after some necessary affairs. Marry, good Sir, in some two years, or less, that the woman has lived here in Boston, no tidings have come of this learned gentleman, Master Prynne; and his young wife, look you, being left to her own misguidance—"

"Aha!—aha!—I understand," said the stranger with a bitter smile. "So learned a man as you speak of should have learned this too in his books. And who, by your favor, Sir, may be the father of yonder babe—it is some three or four months old, I should judge—which Mistress Prynne is holding in her arms?"

---

[1] sojourn: temporary stay

"Of a truth, friend, that matter is a riddle; and the Daniel[2] who shall explain it is yet a-wanting," answered the townsman. "Madam Hester absolutely refuses to speak, and the magistrates have laid their heads together in vain. Peradventure[3] the guilty one stands looking on at the sad spectacle, unknown of man, and forgetting that God sees him."

"The learned man," observed the stranger, with another smile, "should come himself, to look into the mystery."

"It behooves[4] him well if he be still in life," responded the townsman. "Now, good Sir, our Massachusetts magistracy, bethinking themselves that this woman is youthful and fair, and doubtless was strongly tempted to her fall,— and that, moreover, as is most likely, her husband may be at the bottom of the sea,—they have not been bold to be too severe against her. The penalty thereof is death. But in their great mercy and tenderness of heart, they have doomed Mistress Prynne to stand only a space of three hours on the platform of the pillory, and then and thereafter, for the remainder of her natural life, to wear a mark of shame upon her bosom."

"A wise sentence!" remarked the stranger, gravely bowing his head. "Thus she will be a living sermon against sin, until the ignominious[5] letter be engraved upon her tombstone. It irks me, nevertheless, that the partner of her crime should not, at least, stand on the scaffold by her side. But he will be known!—he will be known!—he will be known!"

He bowed to the townsman, and whispering a few

---

[2] Daniel: a Hebrew prophet

[3] peradventure: perhaps

[4] behooves: would be proper for

[5] ignominious: shameful

words to his Indian attendant, they both made their way through the crowd.

While this passed, Hester Prynne had been standing on her pedestal, still with a fixed gaze on the stranger; so fixed a gaze, that all other objects in the visible world seemed to vanish, leaving only him and her. Such an interview, perhaps, would have been more terrible than even to meet him as she now did, with the hot, midday sun burning down upon her face, and lighting up its shame; with the scarlet token of infamy on her breast; with the infant in her arms; with a whole people, drawn forth, as to a festival, staring at the features that should have been seen only in a quiet gleam of the fireside, in the happy shadow of a home, or beneath a matronly veil, at church. Dreadful as it was, she was aware of a shelter in the presence of these thousand witnesses. It was better to stand thus, with so many between him and her, than to greet him, face to face, alone. She fled for refuge, as it were, to the public exposure, and dreaded the moment when its protection should be withdrawn from her. Involved in these thoughts, she scarcely heard a voice behind her, until it had repeated her name more than once, in a loud and solemn tone, audible to the whole crowd.

"Hearken unto me, Hester Prynne!" said the voice.

It has already been noticed, that directly over the platform on which Hester Prynne stood was a kind of balcony, or open gallery, appended to the meeting house. It was the place whence proclamations were made, amidst an assemblage of the magistracy, with all the ceremony that attended such public observances in those days. Here, to witness the scene we are describing, sat Governor Bellingham[6] himself, with four sergeants about his chair, bearing battle-axes, as a guard of honor. He wore a dark

[6] Bellingham: Richard Bellingham (1592–1672), governor of the Massachusetts colony

feather in his hat, a border of embroidery on his cloak, and a black velvet tunic beneath; a gentleman advanced in years, with a hard experience written in his wrinkles. He was not ill-fitted to be the head of a community, which owed its origin and progress, and its present state of development, not to the impulses of youth, but to the stern energies of manhood, and the sombre wisdom of age. The other eminent characters, by whom he was surrounded, were distinguished by a dignity of manner, belonging to a period when the forms of authority were felt to possess the sacredness of Divine institutions. They were, no doubt, good men, just, and sage. But, out of the whole human family, it would not have been easy to select the same number of wise and virtuous persons, who should be less capable of sitting in judgment on an erring woman's heart, and separating its mixture of good and evil, than the sages of rigid aspect towards whom Hester Prynne now turned her face. She seemed conscious, indeed, that whatever sympathy she might expect lay in the larger and warmer heart of the multitude; for, as she lifted her eyes to the balcony, the unhappy woman grew pale and trembled.

The voice which had called her attention was that of the famous John Wilson, the eldest clergyman of Boston, a great scholar, and also a kind and genial man. This last attribute, however, had been less carefully developed than his intellectual gifts, and was, in truth, rather a matter of shame than self-congratulation with him. There he stood, with grizzled locks beneath his skull-cap; while his gray eyes, accustomed to the shaded light of his study, were winking, like those of Hester's infant, in the unadulterated sunshine. He looked like the darkly engraved portraits which we see in old volumes of sermons; and had no more right than one of those portraits would have to step forth, as he now did, and meddle with a question of human guilt, passion, and suffering.

"Hester Prynne," said the clergyman, "I have striven with my young brother here, under whose preaching of the word you have been privileged to sit,"—here Mr. Wilson laid his hand on the shoulder of a pale young man beside him,—"I have sought to persuade this godly youth, that he should deal with you, here in the face of Heaven, and before these wise and upright rulers, and in hearing of all the people, as touching the vileness and blackness of your sin. Knowing your natural temper better than I, he could the better judge what arguments to use, whether of tenderness or terror, that might weaken your hardness and obstinacy; insomuch that you should no longer hide the name of him who tempted you to this grievous fall. But he argues with me that it were wronging the very nature of woman to force her to lay open her heart's secrets in such broad daylight, and in presence of so great a multitude. Truly, as I sought to convince him, the shame lay in committing the sin, and not in showing it forth. What say you to it, once again, Brother Dimmesdale? Must it be thou, or I, that shall deal with this poor sinner's soul?"

There was a murmur among the dignified and reverend occupants of the balcony; and Governor Bellingham gave expression to its purport, speaking in an authoritative voice, although mixed with respect towards the youthful clergyman whom he addressed.

"Good Master Dimmesdale," said he, "the responsibility of this woman's soul lies greatly with you. It behooves you, therefore, to exhort her to repentance, and to confession, as a proof and consequence thereof."

The directness of this appeal drew the eyes of the whole crowd upon the Reverend Mr. Dimmesdale; a young clergyman, who had come from one of the great English universities, bringing all the learning of the age into our wild forest-land. His eloquence and religious fervor had already given promise of high eminence in his profession.

He was a person of very striking aspect, with a white, lofty, and impending brow, large, brown, melancholy eyes, and a mouth which, unless when he forcibly compressed it, was apt to be tremulous, expressing both nervous sensibility and a vast power of self-restraint. Notwithstanding his high native gifts and scholarly attainments, there was an air about this young minister,—a startled, a half-frightened look,—as of a being who felt himself quite astray and at a loss in the pathway of human existence, and could only be at ease in some seclusion of his own. Therefore, so far as his duties would permit, he trod in the shadowy by-paths, and thus kept himself simple and childlike; coming forth, when occasion was, with a freshness, and fragrance, and dewy purity of thought, which, as many people said, affected them like the speech of an angel.

Such was the young man whom the Reverend Mr. Wilson and the Governor had introduced so openly to public notice, bidding him speak, in the hearing of all men, to that mystery of a woman's soul, so sacred even in its shame. The trying nature of his position drove the blood from his cheek, and made his lips tremble.

"Speak to the woman, my brother," said Mr. Wilson. "It is of importance to her soul, and therefore, as the worshipful Governor says, important to thine own, in whose charge hers is. Exhort her to confess the truth!"

The Reverend Mr. Dimmesdale bent his head, in silent prayer, and then came forward.

"Hester Prynne," said he, leaning over the balcony and looking down into her eyes, "thou hearest what this good man says, and seest the accountability under which I labor. If thou feelest it to be for thy soul's peace, and that thy earthly punishment will thereby be made more effectual to salvation, I charge you to speak out the name of your fellow-sinner and fellow-sufferer! Be not silent from any mistaken pity or tenderness for the man; for, believe me,

Hester, though he were to step down from a high place, and stand there beside thee, on thy pedestal of shame, yet better were it so, than to hide a guilty heart through life. What can your silence do for him, except to tempt him—yea, compel him, as it were—to add hypocrisy to sin? Heaven hath granted thee an open ignominy, that thereby thou mayest work out an open triumph over the evil within, and the sorrow without. Take heed how thou deniest to him—who, perchance, hath not the courage to grasp it for himself—the bitter, but wholesome, cup that is now presented to thy lips!"

The young pastor's voice was sweet, rich, deep, and broken. The feeling that it so evidently manifested, rather than the direct purport of the words, caused it to vibrate within all hearts, and brought all the listeners into one accord of sympathy. Even the poor baby, at Hester's bosom, was affected by the same influence; for it directed its hitherto vacant gaze towards Mr. Dimmesdale, and held up its little arms, with a half-pleased, half-plaintive murmur. So powerful was the minister's appeal that the people felt that Hester Prynne would speak out the guilty name; or else that the guilty one himself, in whatever high or lowly place he stood, would be drawn forth by an inward and inevitable necessity, and compelled to ascend the scaffold.

Hester shook her head.

"Woman, sin not beyond the limits of Heaven's mercy!" cried the Reverend Mr. Wilson, more harshly than before. "That little babe hath been gifted with a voice, to second and confirm the counsel which thou hast heard. Speak out the name! That, and thy repentance, may avail to take the scarlet letter off thy breast."

"Never!" replied Hester Prynne, looking, not at Mr. Wilson, but into the deep and troubled eyes of the younger clergyman. "It is too deeply branded. You cannot take it off. And would that I might endure *his* agony, as well!"

"Speak, woman!" said another voice, coldly and sternly, proceeding from the crowd about the scaffold. "Speak; give your child a father!"

"I will not speak!" answered Hester, turning pale as death, but answering this voice, which she too surely recognized. "My child must seek a heavenly Father; she shall never know an earthly one!"

"She will not speak!" murmured Mr. Dimmesdale, who, leaning over the balcony, with his hand upon his heart, had awaited the result of his appeal. "Wonderful strength and generosity of a woman's heart! She will not speak!"

Discerning the impracticable[7] state of the poor culprit's mind, the elder clergyman, who had carefully prepared himself for the occasion, addressed to the multitude a discourse on sin, in all its branches, but with continual reference to the ignominious letter. So forcibly did he dwell upon this symbol, for the hour or more during which his sentences were rolling over the people's heads, that it assumed new terrors in their imagination, and seemed to derive its scarlet hue from the flames of the infernal pit. Hester Prynne, meanwhile, kept her place upon the pedestal of shame, with glazed eyes, and an air of indifference. She had borne, that morning, all that nature could bear; and as her temperament was not the kind that escapes from too intense suffering by fainting, her spirit could only shelter itself beneath a stony crust of insensibility, while her physical faculties remained entire. In this state, the voice of the preacher thundered remorselessly, but unavailingly, upon her ears. The infant, during the latter portion of her ordeal, pierced the air with its wailings and screams; she strove to hush it, mechanically, but seemed scarcely to sympathize with its trouble. With the same hard demeanor, she was led back to prison, and vanished from

[7] impracticable: incapable of being dealt with

the public gaze within its iron-clamped gate. It was whispered, by those who peered after her, that the scarlet letter threw a reddish gleam along the dark passageway of the interior.

4 *The Interview*

After her return to the prison, Hester Prynne was found to be in a state of nervous excitement that demanded constant watchfulness lest she should harm herself, or her child. As night approached, it proving impossible to quell her insubordination by rebuke or threats of punishment, Master Brackett, the jailer, thought fit to introduce a physician. He described him as a man of skill in all Christian modes of physical science, and likewise familiar with whatever the savage people could teach, in respect to medicinal herbs and roots that grew in the forest. To say the truth, there was much need of professional assistance, not merely for Hester herself, but still more urgently for the child; who, drawing its milk from the maternal bosom, seemed to have drunk in with it all the turmoil, the anguish and despair, which pervaded the mother's system. It now writhed in convulsions, and was a forcible type[1] in its little frame, of the moral agony which Hester Prynne had borne throughout the day.

Closely following the jailer into the dismal apartment appeared that individual whose presence in the crowd had been of such deep interest to the wearer of the scarlet letter. He was lodged in the prison, not as suspected of any offence, but as the most convenient and suitable mode of

[1] type: visible form or symbol

disposing of him, until the magistrate should have conferred with the Indian chiefs respecting his ransom. His name was announced as Roger Chillingworth. The jailer, after ushering him into the room, remained a moment, marvelling at the comparative quiet that followed his entrance; for Hester Prynne had immediately become as still as death, although the child continued to moan.

"Prithee, friend, leave me alone with my patient," said the physician. "Trust me, good jailer, you shall briefly have peace in your house; and, I promise you, Mistress Prynne shall hereafter be more agreeable to just authority than you may have found her heretofore."

"Nay, if your worship can accomplish that," answered Master Brackett, "I shall own you for a man of skill indeed! Verily, the woman hath been like a possessed one; and there lacks little, that I should take in hand to drive Satan out of her with stripes."

The stranger had entered the room with the characteristic quietude of the profession to which he announced himself as belonging. Nor did his manner change, when the withdrawal of the prison-keeper left him face to face with the woman, whose absorbed notice of him, in the crowd, had intimated so close a relation between himself and her. His first care was given to the child; whose cries, indeed, as she lay writhing on the low bed, made it of absolute necessity to postpone all other business to the task of soothing her. He examined the infant carefully, and then proceeded to unclasp a leathern case, which he took from beneath his dress. It appeared to contain medical preparations, one of which he mingled with a cup of water.

"My old studies in alchemy,"[2] observed he, "and my sojourn, for above a year past, among a people well versed in the kindly properties of plants, have made a better physician of me than many that claim the medical degree.

[2] alchemy: medieval chemistry, as opposed to modern science

Here, woman! The child is yours,—she is none of mine,—neither will she recognize my voice or aspect as a father's. Give her this medicine, therefore, with thine own hand."

Hester repelled the offered medicine, at the same time gazing with strongly marked fear into his face.

"Wouldst thou avenge thyself on an innocent babe?" whispered she.

"Foolish woman!" responded the physician, half coldly, half soothingly. "What should ail me, to harm this misbegotten and miserable babe? The medicine is powerful for good; and were it *my* child,—yea, mine own, as well as thine!—I could do no better for it."

As she still hesitated, being, in fact, in no reasonable state of mind, he took the infant in his arms, and himself administered the draught. It soon proved its efficacy,[3] and redeemed the doctor's pledge. The moans of the little patient subsided; its convulsive tossings gradually ceased; and, in a few moments, as is the custom of young children after relief from pain, it sank into a profound and dewy slumber. The physician next bestowed his attention on the mother. With calm and intent scrutiny, he felt her pulse, looked into her eyes,—a gaze that made her heart shrink and shudder, because so familiar, and yet so strange and cold,—and, finally, satisfied with his investigation, proceeded to mingle another draught.

"I learned not how to make thee forget," remarked he, "but I have learned many new secrets in the wilderness, and here is one of them,—a recipe that an Indian taught me, in requital of[4] some lessons of my own, that were as old as Paracelsus.[5] Drink it! It may be less soothing than a sinless conscience. That I cannot give thee. But it will

---

[3] efficacy: effectiveness

[4] in requital of: in return for

[5] Paracelsus: a famous Swiss alchemist and doctor (1493–1541)

calm the swell and heaving of thy passion, like oil thrown on the waves of a tempestuous sea."

He presented the cup to Hester, who received it with a slow, earnest look into his face; not precisely a look of fear, yet full of doubt and questioning, as to his purposes might be. She looked also at her slumbering child.

"I have thought of death," said she,—"have wished for it,—would even have prayed for it, were it fit that such as I should pray for anything. Yet, if death be in this cup, I bid thee think again, ere thou beholdest me quaff it. See! It is even now at my lips."

"Drink, then," replied he, still with the same cold composure. "Dost thou know me so little, Hester Prynne? Are my purposes wont to be so shallow? Even if I imagine a scheme of vengeance, what could I do better for my object than to let thee live,—than to give thee medicines against all harm and peril of life,—so that this burning shame may still blaze upon thy bosom?" As he spoke, he laid his long forefinger on the scarlet letter, which forthwith seemed to scorch into Hester's breast, as if it had been red-hot. He noticed her involuntary gesture, and smiled. "Live, therefore, and bear about thy doom with thee, in the eyes of men and women,—in the eyes of him whom thou call thy husband,—in the eyes of yonder child! And, that thou mayest live, drink this draught."

Without further delay, Hester Prynne drained the cup, and, at the motion of the man of skill, seated herself on the bed where the child was sleeping; while he drew the only chair which the room afforded, and took his own seat beside her. She could not but tremble at these preparations; for she felt that—having now done all that humanity, or principle, or, if so it were, a refined cruelty, impelled him to do, for the relief of physical suffering—he was next to treat with her as the man whom she had most deeply injured.

"Hester," said he, "I ask not wherefore, nor how, thou hast fallen into the pit, or say, rather, thou hast ascended to the pedestal of infamy, on which I found thee. The reason is not far to seek. It was my folly, and thy weakness. I,—a man of thought, the bookworm of great libraries,—a man already in decay, having given my best years to feed the hungry dream of knowledge,—what had I to do with youth and beauty like thine own! Misshapen from my birth, how could I fool myself with the idea that intellectual gifts might hide physical deformity in a young girl's fantasy! Men call me wise. If sages were ever wise in their own interest, I might have foreseen all this. I might have known that, as I came out of the vast and dismal forest, and entered this settlement of Christian men, the very first object to meet my eyes would be thyself, Hester Prynne, standing up, a statue of shame, before the people. Nay, from the moment when we came down the old church steps together, a married pair, I might have beheld the fire of that scarlet letter blazing at the end of our path!"

"Thou knowest," said Hester,—for, depressed as she was, she could not endure this last quiet stab at the token of her shame,—"thou knowest that I was frank with thee. I felt no love, nor pretended any."

"True," replied he. "It was my folly! I have said it. But, up to that epoch of my life, I had lived in vain. The world had been so cheerless! My heart was a home large enough for many guests, but lonely and chill, and without a household fire. I longed to kindle one! It seemed not so wild a dream,—old as I was, and gloomy as I was, and misshapen as I was,—that the simple bliss, which is scattered far and wide, for all mankind to gather up, might yet be mine. And so, Hester, I drew thee into my heart, into its innermost chamber, and sought to warm thee by the warmth which thy presence made there!"

"I have greatly wronged thee," murmured Hester.

"We have wronged each other," answered he. "Mine was the first wrong, when I betrayed thy budding youth into a false and unnatural relation with my old age. There- fore, as a man who has not thought in vain, I seek no vengeance, plot no evil against *thee*. Between thee and me, the scale hangs fairly balanced. But, Hester, the man lives who has wronged us both! Who is he?"

"Ask me not!" replied Hester Prynne, looking firmly into his face. "*That* thou shalt never know!"

"Never, sayest thou?" rejoined he, with a smile of dark and self-relying intelligence. "Never know him! Believe me, Hester, there are few things hidden from the man who devotes himself earnestly and unreservedly to the solution of a mystery. Thou mayest cover up thy secret from the prying multitude. Thou mayest conceal it, too, from min- isters and magistrates, even as thou didst this day, when they sought to wrench the name out of thy heart, and give thee a partner on thy pedestal. But, as for me, I come to the inquest with other senses than they possess. I shall seek this man, as I have sought truth in books. There is a sympathy[6] that will make me conscious of him. I shall see him tremble. I shall feel myself shudder, suddenly and unawares. Sooner or later, he must needs be mine!"

The eyes of the wrinkled scholar glowed so intensely upon her, that Hester Prynne clasped her hands over her heart, dreading lest the old man should read the secret there at once.

"Thou wilt not reveal his name? Not the less he is mine," resumed he, with a look of confidence. "He bears no letter of infamy wrought into his garment, as thou dost; but I shall read it on his heart. Yet fear not for him! Think not that I shall interfere with Heaven's own method of punishment, or, to my own loss, betray him to the clutch of human law. Neither do thou imagine that I shall contrive

[6] sympathy: special instinct

aught against his life; no, nor against his reputation, if, as I judge, he be a man of fair repute. Let him live! Let him hide himself in *outward* honor, if he may! Not the less he shall be mine!"

"Thy acts are like mercy," said Hester, bewildered and appalled. "But thy words make thee a terror!"

"One thing, thou that wast my wife, I would enjoin upon thee," continued the scholar. "Thou hast kept the secret of thy lover. Keep, likewise, mine! There are none in this land that know me. Breathe not, to any human soul, that thou didst ever call me husband! Here, on this wild outskirt of the earth, I shall pitch my tent; for, elsewhere a wanderer, and isolated from human interests, I find here a woman, a man, a child, amongst whom and myself there exist the closest ties. No matter whether of love or hate; no matter whether of right or wrong! Thou and thine, Hester Prynne, belong to me. My home is where thou art, and where he is. But betray me not!"

"Wherefore[7] dost thou desire it?" inquired Hester, shrinking, she hardly knew why, from this secret bond. "Why not announce thyself openly, and cast me off at once?"

"It may be," he replied, "because I will not encounter the dishonor that stains the husband of a faithless woman. It may be for other reasons. Enough, that it is my purpose to live and die unknown. Let, therefore, thy husband be to the world as one already dead, and of whom no news shall ever come. Recognize me not, by word, by sign, by look! Breathe not the secret, above all, to the man thou knowest of. Shouldst thou fail me in this, beware! His fame, his position, his life, will be in my hands. Beware!"

"I will keep thy secret, as I have his," said Hester.

"Swear it!" rejoined he.

"I swear," she answered quietly.

[7] wherefore: why

"And now, Mistress Prynne," said old Roger Chilling-worth, as he was hereafter to be named, "I leave thee alone; alone with thy infant, and the scarlet letter! How is it, Hester? Doth thy sentence bind thee to wear the token in thy sleep? Art thou not afraid of nightmares and hideous dreams?"

"Why dost thou smile so at me?" inquired Hester, troubled at the expression of his eyes. "Art thou like the Black Man[8] that haunts the forest round about us? Hast thou enticed me into a bond that will prove the ruin of my soul?"

"Not *thy* soul," he answered, with another smile. "No, not *thine!*"

---

[8] Black Man: Satan, or the devil

5 *Hester at Her Needle*

Hester Prynne's term of confinement was now at an end. Her prison-door was thrown open, and she came forth into the sunshine, which, falling on all alike, seemed, to her sick heart, as if meant for no other purpose than to reveal the scarlet letter on her breast. Perhaps there was a more real torture in her first unattended footsteps from the threshold of the prison, than even in the procession and spectacle that have been described, where she was made the common shame, at which all mankind was summoned to point its finger. Then, she was supported by an unnatural tension of the nerves, and by all the fighting energy of her character, which enabled her to convert the scene into a kind of triumph. It was, moreover, a separate event, to occur but once in her lifetime, and to meet which, therefore, she might call up the vital strength that would have sufficed for many quiet years. The very law that condemned her had held her up, through the terrible ordeal of her ignominy.[1] But now, with this unattended walk from her prison-door, began the daily custom; and she must either bear and carry it forward by the ordinary resources of her nature, or sink beneath it. She could no longer borrow from the future to help her through the present grief. To-morrow would bring its own trial with it;

[1] ignominy: shame, dishonor

so would the next day, and the next; each its own trial, and yet the very same that was now so unutterably grievous to be borne. The days of the far-off future would toil onward, still with the same burden for her to take up, and bear along with her, but never to fling down; for the accumulating days, and added years, would pile up their misery upon the heap of shame. Throughout them all, giving up her individuality, she would become the general symbol at which the preacher and moralist might point, and in which they might vivify[2] and embody their images of woman's frailty and sinful passion. Thus the young and pure would be taught to look at her, with the scarlet letter flaming on her breast,—*at her,* the child of honorable parents,—*at her,* the mother of a babe, that would hereafter be a woman,—*at her,* who had once been innocent,—as the figure, the body, the reality of sin. And over her grave, the shame that she must carry thither would be her only monument.

It may seem marvellous, with the world before her, that this woman should still call that place her home, where, and where only, she must needs be the type of shame. But there is a fatality, a feeling so irresistible and inevitable that it has the force of doom, which almost invariably compels human beings to linger around and haunt the spot where some great and marked event has given the color to their lifetime; and still the more irresistibly, the darker the tinge that saddens it. Her sin, her ignominy, were the roots which she had struck into the soil. It was as if a new birth, with stronger ties than the first, had converted the forest-land, still so uncongenial to every other pilgrim and wanderer, into Hester Prynne's wild and dreary but lifelong home. All other scenes of earth—even the village of rural England, where happy infancy and stainless maidenhood seemed yet to be in her

---

[2] vivify: make more vivid

mother's keeping, like garments put off long ago—were foreign to her, in comparison. The chain that bound her here was of iron links, and galling to her inmost soul, but it could never be broken.

It might be, too,—doubtless it was so, although she hid the secret from herself, and grew pale whenever it struggled out of her heart,—it might be that another feeling kept her within the scene and pathway that had been so fatal. There dwelt, there trod the feet of one with whom she deemed herself connected in a union, that, unrecognized on earth, would bring them together before the bar of final judgment, and make that their marriage-altar, for a joint futurity of endless retribution. Over and over again, the tempter of souls had thrust this idea upon Hester, and laughed at the passionate and desperate joy with which she seized and then strove to cast it from her. She barely looked the idea in the face, and hastened to bar it in its dungeon. What she compelled herself to believe—what, finally, she reasoned upon, as her motive for continuing a resident of New England—was half a truth, and half a self-delusion. Here, she said to herself, had been the scene of her guilt, and here should be the scene of her earthly punishment; and so, perchance, the torture of her daily shame would at length purge her soul, and work out another purity than that which she had lost; more saint-like, because the result of martyrdom.

Hester Prynne, therefore, did not flee. On the outskirts of the town there was a small thatched cottage. It had been built by an earlier settler, and abandoned, because the soil about it was too sterile for cultivation, while its comparative remoteness put it out of the sphere of that social activity which already marked the habits of the emigrants. It stood on the shore, looking across a basin of the sea at the forest-covered hills, towards the west. A clump of scrubby trees, such as alone grew on the peninsula, did not so much conceal the cottage from view, as seem to denote that here was some object which ought to be concealed. In this little, lonesome dwelling, with some slender means that she possessed, and by the license of the magistrates, who still kept a sharp watch over her, Hester established herself, with her child. A mystic shadow of suspicion immediately attached itself to the spot. Children, too young to understand why this woman should be shut out from the sphere of human charities, would creep near enough to behold her plying her needle at the cottage-window, or standing at the doorway, or laboring in her little garden, or coming forth along the pathway that led townward; and seeing the scarlet letter on her breast, would scamper off.

Lonely as was Hester's situation, and without a friend on earth who dared to show himself, she, however, was in no danger of want. She possessed an art that sufficed, even in a land that afforded comparatively little scope for its exercise, to supply food for her infant and herself. It was the art—then, as now, almost the only one within a woman's grasp—of needlework. She bore on her breast, in the curiously embroidered letter, a specimen of her skill, of which the dames of a court might gladly have availed themselves, to add the richer and more spiritual adornment of human ingenuity to their fabrics of silk and gold. Here, indeed, in the sable simplicity that generally characterized the Puritanic modes of dress, there might be an infrequent call for the finer productions of her handiwork. Yet the taste of the age, demanding whatever was elaborate in compositions of this kind, did not fail to extend its influence over our stern ancestors who had cast behind them so many fashions which it might seem harder to dispense with. Public ceremonies, such as ordinations, the installation of magistrates, and all that could give majesty to the forms in which a new government manifested itself to the people, were, as a matter of policy, marked by a stately and

well-conducted ceremonial, and a sombre, but yet a studied magnificence. Deep ruffs, painfully wrought bands, and gorgeously embroidered gloves, were all deemed necessary to the official state of men holding the reins of power; and were readily allowed to individuals dignified by rank or wealth, even while strict laws forbade these and similar extravagances to the common people. In the array of funerals, too,—whether for the apparel of the dead body, or to typify the sorrow of the survivors,—there was a frequent demand for such labor as Hester Prynne could supply. Baby-linen—for babies then wore robes of state—afforded still another possibility of toil and profit.

By degrees, nor very slowly, her handiwork became what would now be termed the fashion. Whether from pity for a woman of so miserable a fate; or from the morbid curiosity that gives a fictitious value even to common or worthless things; or by whatever other intangible circumstance was then, as now, enough to bestow, on some persons, what others might seek in vain; or because Hester really filled a gap which must otherwise have remained vacant; it is certain that she had ready and fairly paid employment for as many hours as she saw fit to occupy with her needle. Vanity, it may be, chose to mortify itself, by putting on, for ceremonies of pomp and state, the garments that had been wrought by her sinful hands. Her needlework was seen on the ruff of the Governor; military men wore it on their scarfs, and the minister on his band; it decked the baby's little cap; it was shut up to moulder away, in the coffins of the dead. But it is not recorded that her skill was called in aid to embroider the white veil which was to cover the pure blushes of a bride. The exception indicated the ever-relentless rigor with which society frowned upon her sin.

Hester sought not to acquire anything beyond a living, of the plainest and simplest description, for herself, and a simple abundance for her child. Her own dress was of the coarsest materials and the most sombre hue; with only that one ornament,—the scarlet letter,—which it was her doom to wear. The child's attire, on the other hand, was distinguished by a fanciful, or, we might rather say, a fantastic ingenuity, which served, indeed, to heighten the airy charm that early began to develop itself in the little girl, but which appeared to have also a deeper meaning. Except for that small expenditure in the decoration of her infant, Hester bestowed all her superfluous means in char- ity, on wretches less miserable than herself, and who not infrequently insulted the hand that fed them. Much of the time, which she might readily have applied to the better efforts of her art, she employed in making coarse garments for the poor. It is probable that there was an idea of penance in this mode of occupation, and that she offered up a real sacrifice of enjoyment, in devoting so many hours to such rude handiwork. Women derive a pleasure, incomprehen- sible to the other sex, from the delicate toil of the needle. To Hester Prynne it might have been a mode of expressing, and therefore soothing, the passion of her life. Like all other joys, she rejected it as sin.

In this manner, Hester Prynne came to have a part to perform in the world. With her native energy of character, and rare capacity, it could not entirely cast her off, although it had set a mark upon her, more intolerable to a woman's heart than that which branded the brow of Cain.[3] In all her dealings with society, however, there was nothing that made her feel as if she belonged to it. Every gesture, every word, and even the silence of those with whom she came in contact, implied, and often expressed, that she was banished, and as much alone as if she inhabited another

[3] Cain: the first son of Adam and Eve, and the slayer of his brother, Abel

sphere, or communicated with the common nature by other organs and senses than the rest of human kind. She stood apart from moral interests, yet close beside them, like a ghost that revisits the familiar fireside, and can no longer make itself seen or felt; no more smile with the household joy, nor mourn with the kindred sorrow; or, should it succeed in showing its forbidden sympathy, awakening only terror. These emotions, in fact, and its bitterest scorn besides, seemed to be the sole portion that she retained in the universal heart. It was not an age of delicacy; and her position, although she understood it well, and was in little danger of forgetting it, was often brought before her, like a new anguish, by the rudest touch upon the tenderest spot. The poor, as we have already said, whom she sought out to be the objects of her bounty, often reviled[4] the hand that was stretched forth to help them. Dames of elevated rank, likewise, whose doors she entered in the way of her occupation, were accustomed to distil drops of bitterness into her heart, sometimes through that alchemy of quiet malice, by which women can make a subtle poison from ordinary trifles; and sometimes, also, by a coarser expression, that fell upon the sufferer's defenceless breast like a rough blow upon an open wound. Hester had schooled herself long and well; she never responded to these attacks, save by a flush of crimson that rose over her pale cheek, and again subsided into the depths of her bosom. She was patient,—a martyr, indeed,—but she did not pray for her enemies; lest, in spite of her forgiving aspirations, the words of the prayer should twist themselves into a curse.

Continually, and in a thousand other ways, did she feel the innumerable throbs of anguish that had been so cunningly contrived for her by the undying, the ever-active sentence of the Puritan tribunal. Clergymen paused in the

---

[4] reviled: spoke badly of

street to address words of exhortation, that brought a crowd, with its mingled grin and frown, around the poor, sinful woman. If she entered a church, trusting to share the Sabbath smile of the Universal Father, it was often her mishap to find herself the text of the sermon. She grew to dread children; for they had imbibed[5] from their parents a vague idea of something horrible in this dreary woman, gliding silently through the town, with never any companion but her own child. Therefore, first allowing her to pass, they pursued her at a distance with shrill cries, and the utterance of a word that had no distinct meaning to their own minds, but was none the less terrible to her, as coming from lips that babbled it unconsciously. It seemed to argue so wide a diffusion of her shame, that all nature knew of it; it could have caused her no deeper pang, had the leaves of the trees whispered the dark story among themselves,— had the summer breeze murmured about it,—had the wintry blast shrieked it aloud! Another peculiar torture was felt in the gaze of a new eye. When strangers looked curiously at the scarlet letter, they branded it afresh into Hester's soul; so that oftentimes, she could scarcely refrain, yet always did refrain, from covering the symbol with her hand. But then, again, an accustomed eye had likewise its own anguish to inflict. Its cool stare of familiarity was intolerable. From first to last, in short, Hester Prynne had always this dreadful agony in feeling a human eye upon the token; the spot never grew callous; it seemed, on the contrary, to grow more sensitive with daily torture.

Her imagination was somewhat affected, and, had she been of a softer moral and intellectual fibre, would have been still more so, by the strange and solitary anguish of her life. Walking to and fro, with those lonely footsteps, in the little world with which she was outwardly connected, it now and then appeared to Hester that the scarlet letter

---

[5] had imbibed: had taken in from

had endowed her with a new sense. She shuddered to believe, yet could not help believing, that it gave her a sympathetic knowledge of the hidden sin in other hearts. She was terror-stricken by the revelations that were thus made. What were they? Could they be other than the insidious whispers of the bad angel, who would have persuaded the struggling woman, as yet only half his victim, that the outward guise of purity was but a lie, and that, if truth were everywhere to be shown, a scarlet letter would blaze forth on many a bosom besides Hester Prynne's? Sometimes the red infamy upon her breast would give a sympathetic throb, as she passed near a venerable minister or magistrate, the model of piety and justice, to whom that age of antique reverence looked up, as to a mortal man in fellowship with angels. "What evil thing is at hand?" Hester would say to herself. Looking up there would be nothing human within the scope of view, save the form of this earthly saint! Again, a mystic sisterhood would rebelliously assert itself, as she met the sanctified frown of some matron, who, according to the rumor of all tongues, had kept cold snow within her bosom throughout life. That unsunned snow in the matron's bosom, and the burning shame on Hester Prynne's,—what had the two in common? Or, once more, the electric thrill would give her warning,—"Behold, Hester, here is a companion!"—and, looking up, she would detect the eyes of a young maiden glancing at the scarlet letter, shyly and aside, and quickly averted with a faint, chill crimson in her cheeks; as if her purity were somewhat sullied by that momentary glance.

The vulgar, who, in those dreary old times, were always contributing a grotesque horror to what interested their imaginations, had a story about the scarlet letter which we might readily work up into a terrific legend. They averred, that the symbol was not mere scarlet cloth, but was red-hot with an infernal fire, and could be seen glowing all alight, whenever Hester Prynne walked abroad in the nighttime. And we must needs say, it seared Hester's bosom so deeply, that perhaps there was more truth in the rumor than our modern doubt may be willing to admit.

⑥ *Pearl*

We have as yet hardly spoken of the infant; that little creature, whose innocent life had sprung, by the mysterious decree of Providence, a lovely and immortal flower, out of the rank luxuriance of a guilty passion. How strange it seemed to the sad woman, as she watched the growth, and the beauty that became every day more brilliant, and the intelligence that threw its quivering sunshine over the tiny features of this child! Her Pearl!—For so had Hester called her; not as a name expressive of her aspect, which had nothing of the calm, white lustre that would be indicated by the comparison. But she named the infant "Pearl," as being of great price—purchased with all she had,—her mother's only treasure! How strange, indeed! Man had marked this woman's sin by a scarlet letter, which had such potent efficacy that no human sympathy could reach her, save it were sinful like herself. God, as a direct consequence of the sin which man thus punished, had given her a lovely child, whose place was on that same dishonored bosom, to connect her parent forever with the race and descent of mortals, and to be finally a blessed soul in heaven! Yet these thoughts affected Hester Prynne less with hope than apprehension. She knew that her deed had been evil; she could have no faith, therefore, that its result would be good. Day after day, she looked fearfully into the child's expanding nature, ever dreading to detect some dark and wild peculiarity, that should correspond with the guilt to which she owed her being.

Certainly, there was no physical defect. The child had a native grace which does not always coexist with faultless beauty; its attire, however simple, always impressed the beholder as if it were the very garb that precisely became it best. But little Pearl was not clad in rustic weeds. Her mother, with a morbid purpose, had bought the richest tissues that could be procured, and allowed her imagination its full play in the arrangement and decoration of the dresses which the child wore. So magnificent was the small figure, when thus dressed, and such was the splendor of Pearl's own beauty, shining through the gorgeous robes which might have extinguished a paler loveliness, that there existed an absolute circle of radiance around her, on the dark cottage floor. And yet a reddish gown, torn and soiled with the child's rude play, made a picture just as perfect. Pearl's aspect was imbued with a spell of infinite variety; in this one child there were many children, comprehending the full scope between the wild flower prettiness of a peasant-baby, and the pomp of an infant princess. Throughout all, however, there was a passion, a certain depth of hue, which she never lost; and if, in any of her changes, she had grown fainter or paler, she would have ceased to be herself,—to be Pearl.

This outward mutability[1] indicated, and did no more than fairly express, the various properties of her inner life. Her nature appeared to possess depth, too, as well as variety; but—or else Hester's fears deceived her—it lacked reference and adaptation to the world into which she was born. The child could not be made amenable to rules. In giving her existence, a great law had been broken; and the result was a being whose elements were beautiful and

[1] mutability: changeableness

brilliant, perhaps, but all in disorder; or with an order peculiar to themselves, amidst which the point of variety and arrangement was difficult to be discovered. Hester could only account for the child's character—and even then only vaguely—by recalling what she herself had been, during that momentous period while Pearl was imbibing her soul from the spiritual world, and her bodily frame from its material of earth. The mother's impassioned state had been the medium through which were transmitted to the unborn infant the rays of its moral life; and, however white and clear originally, they had taken the deep stains of crimson and gold, the fiery lustre, the black shadow, and the untempered light of the intervening substance. Above all, the warfare of Hester's spirit, at that epoch, was perpetuated in Pearl. She could recognize her wild, desperate, defiant mood, the flightiness of her temper, and even some of the very cloud-shapes of gloom and despondency that had brooded in her heart.

The discipline of the family, in those days, was far more rigid than now. The frown, the harsh rebuke, the frequent application of the rod, ordered by Scriptural authority, were used, not merely as punishment for actual offences, but as a wholesome regimen for the growth of all childish virtues. Hester Prynne, nevertheless, the lonely mother of this child, ran little risk of erring on the side of undue severity. Mindful, however, of her own errors and misfortunes, she early sought to impose a tender, but strict, control over the infant immortality committed to her charge. But the task was beyond her skill. After testing both smiles and frowns, and proving that neither mode of treatment possessed any great influence, Hester was finally compelled to stand aside, and permit the child to be swayed by her own impulses. Physical force was effectual, of course, while it lasted. As to any other kind of discipline, whether addressed to her mind or heart, little Pearl might or might not be within its reach, in accordance with the mood of the moment. Her mother, while Pearl was yet an infant, grew acquainted with a certain peculiar look, that warned her when it would be labor wasted to insist, persuade, or plead. It was a look so intelligent, yet inexplicable, so perverse, sometimes so malicious, but generally accompanied by a wild flow of spirits, that Hester could not help questioning, at such moments, whether Pearl were human. She seemed rather an airy sprite, which, after playing its fantastic sports for a little while upon the cottage floor, would flit away with a mocking smile. Whenever that look appeared in her wild, bright, black eyes, it invested her with a strange remoteness and intangibility;[2] it was as if she were hovering in the air and might vanish, like a glimmering light that comes we know not whence, and goes we know not whither. Beholding it, Hester would rush towards the child,—to pursue the little elf in her flight—to snatch her to her bosom, with hugs and earnest kisses,—not so much from overflowing love, as to assure herself that Pearl was flesh and blood. But Pearl's laugh, when she was caught, though full of merriment and music, made her mother more doubtful than before.

Heart-smitten at this bewildering and baffling spell, that so often came between herself and her sole treasure, whom she had bought so dear, and who was all her world, Hester sometimes burst into passionate tears. Then, perhaps,—for there was no foreseeing how it might affect her,—Pearl would frown, clench her little fist, and harden her small features into a stern, unsympathizing look of discontent. Not seldom, she would laugh anew, and louder than before, like a thing incapable and unintelligent of human sorrow. Or—but this more rarely happened—she would be convulsed with a rage of grief, and sob out her love for her mother in broken words, and seem intent on

[2] intangibility: lack of bodily substance

proving that she had a heart, by breaking it. Yet Hester was hardly safe in confiding herself to that tenderness; it passed as suddenly as it came. Brooding over all these matters, the mother felt like one who has evoked a spirit, but, by some irregularity in the process of conjuration, has failed to win the master-word that should control this new and incomprehensible intelligence. Her only real comfort was when the child lay in the placidity of sleep. Then she was sure of her, and tasted hours of quiet, delicious happiness; until—perhaps with that perverse expression glimmering from beneath her opening lids—little Pearl awoke!

How soon—with what strange rapidity, indeed!—did Pearl arrive at an age that was capable of social intercourse, beyond the mother's ever-ready smile and nonsense-words! And then what a happiness would it have been could Hester Prynne have heard her clear, bird-like voice mingling with other childish voices, and have distinguished her own darling's tones, amid all the entangled outcry of a group of sportive children! But this could never be. Pearl was a born outcast of the infantile world. An imp of evil, emblem and product of sin, she had no right among christened infants. Nothing was more remarkable than the instinct, as it seemed, with which the child comprehended her loneliness; the destiny that had drawn an inviolable circle round about her; the whole peculiarity, in short, of her position in respect to other children. Never, since her release from prison, had Hester met the public gaze without her. In all her walks about the town, Pearl, too, was there; first as a babe in arms, and afterwards as a little girl, small companion of her mother, holding a forefinger with her whole grasp, and tripping along at the rate of three or four steps to one of Hester's. She saw the children of the settlement, on the grassy margin of the street, or at the domestic thresholds, playing in such grim fashion as the Puritanic code would permit; playing at going to church, perchance;

or at scourging Quakers; or taking scalps in a sham-fight with Indians; or scaring one another with freaks of imitative witchcraft. Pearl saw, and gazed intently, but never sought to make acquaintance. If spoken to, she would not speak again. If the children gathered about her, as they sometimes did, Pearl would grow positively terrible in her puny wrath, snatching up stones to fling at them, with shrill, incoherent cries, that made her mother tremble because they had so much the sound of a witch's curses in some unknown tongue.

The truth was, that the little Puritans, being of the most intolerant brood that ever lived, had a vague idea of something outlandish, unearthly, or at odds with ordinary fashions, in the mother and child; and therefore scorned them in their hearts, and not infrequently reviled them with their tongues. Pearl felt the sentiment, and returned it with the bitterest hatred that can be supposed to rankle in a childish bosom. These outbreaks of a fierce temper had a kind of value, and even comfort, for her mother; because there was at least an understandable earnestness in the mood, instead of the fitful caprice that so often thwarted her in the child's manifestations. It appalled her, nevertheless, to discern here, again, a shadowy reflection of the evil that had existed in herself. All this enmity and passion had Pearl inherited, by inalienable right, out of Hester's heart.

At home, within and around her mother's cottage, Pearl did not lack a wide and various circle of acquaintance. The spell of life went forth from her ever-creative spirit, and communicated itself to a thousand objects, as a torch kindles a flame. The unlikeliest materials—a stick, a bunch of rags, a flower—were the puppets, of Pearl's witchcraft, and, without undergoing any outward change, became spiritually adapted to whatever drama occupied the stage of her inner world. Her one baby-voice served a

multitude of imaginary personages, old and young, to talk withal. The pine-trees, aged, black, and solemn, and flinging groans and other melancholy utterances on the breeze, needed little transformation to become Puritan elders; the ugliest weeds of the garden were their children, whom Pearl smote down and uprooted, most unmercifully. It was wonderful, the vast variety of forms into which she threw her intellect, with no continuity, indeed, but darting up and dancing, always in a state of preternatural[3] activity,— soon sinking down, as if exhausted by so rapid and feverish a tide of life, and succeeded by other shapes of a similar wild energy. It was like nothing so much as the changing shifting play of the northern lights.[4] In the mere exercise of the fancy, however, and the sportiveness of a growing mind, there might be little more than was observable in other children of bright faculties; except as Pearl, in the lack of human playmates, was thrown more upon the imaginary throng which she created. The strangeness lay in the bitter feelings with which the child regarded all these offspring of her own heart and mind. She never created a friend, but seemed always to be sowing broadcast the dragon's teeth,[5] whence sprung a harvest of armed enemies, against whom she rushed to battle. It was inexpressibly said—then what depth of sorrow to a mother, who felt in her own heart the cause!—to observe, in one so young, this constant recognition of an unfriendly world, and so fierce a training of the energies that were to make good her cause in the contest that must ensue.

Gazing at Pearl, Hester often dropped her work upon her knees, and cried out with an agony which she would fain have hidden, but which made utterance for itself,

[3] preternatural: more than normal

[4] northern lights: bands of light in the sky near the North Pole; also called the Aurora Borealis

[5] dragon's teeth: a reference to the story, in Greek mythology

betwixt speech and a groan,—"O Father in Heaven,—if Thou art still my Father,—what is this being which I have brought into the world!" And Pearl, overhearing the cry, or aware of those throbs of anguish, would turn her vivid and beautiful little face upon her mother, smile with a sprite-like intelligence, and resume her play.

One peculiarity of the child's conduct remains to be told. The very first thing which she had noticed in her life was—what?—not the mother's smile, responding to it, as other babies do, by that faint, embryo smile of the little mouth, remembered so doubtfully afterwards, and with such fond discussion whether it were indeed a smile. By no means! But that *first* object of which Pearl seemed to become aware was—shall we say it?—the scarlet letter on Hester's bosom! One day, as her mother stooped over the cradle, the infant's eyes had been caught by the glimmering of the gold embroidery about the letter; and, putting up her little hand, she grasped at it, smiling not doubtfully, but with a decided gleam, that gave her face the look of a much older child. Then, gasping for breath, did Hester Prynne clutch the fatal token, instinctively endeavoring to tear it away; so infinite was the torture inflicted by the touch of Pearl's baby-hand. Again, as if her mother's agonized gesture were meant only to make sport for her, did little Pearl look into her eyes, and smile! From that time, except when she was asleep, Hester had never felt a moment's safety; not a moment's calm enjoyment of her. Weeks, it is true, would sometimes pass, during which Pearl's gaze might never once be fixed upon the scarlet letter; but then, again, it would come at unawares, like the stroke of sudden death, and always with that peculiar smile, and odd expression of the eyes.

Once, this freakish, elfish cast came into the child's eyes, while Hester was looking at her own image in them, as mothers are fond of doing; and suddenly she fancied that she beheld, not her own miniature portrait, but an-other face, in the small black mirror of Pearl's eyes. It was a face, fiend-like, full of smiling malice, yet bearing the semblance of features that she had known full well, though seldom with a smile, and never with malice in them. It was as if an evil spirit possessed the child, and had just then peeped forth in mockery. Many a time afterwards had Hester been tortured, though less vividly, by the same illusion.

In the afternoon of a certain summer's day, after Pearl grew big enough to run about, she amused herself with gathering handfuls of wild flowers, and flinging them, one by one, at her mother's bosom; dancing up and down, like a little elf, whenever she hit the scarlet letter. Hester's first motion had been to cover her bosom with her clasped hands. But, whether from pride or resignation, or a feeling that her penance might best be wrought out by this un-utterable pain, she resisted the impulse, and sat erect, pale as death, looking sadly into little Pearl's wild eyes. Still came the battery of flowers, almost always hitting the mark, and covering the mother's breast with hurts for which she could find no balm in this world, nor knew how to seek it in another. At last, her shot being all expended, the child stood still and gazed at Hester, with that little, laughing image of a fiend peeping out—or, whether it peeped or no, her mother so imagined it—from the un-searchable abyss of her black eyes.

"Child, what art thou?" cried the mother.

"Oh, I am your little Pearl!" answered the child.

But, while she said it, Pearl laughed, and began to dance up and down, with the humorsome gesticulation of an imp whose next freak might be to fly up the chimney.

"Art thou my child, in very truth?" asked Hester.

Nor did she put the question altogether idly, but, for the moment, with genuine earnestness; for, such was

Pearl's wonderful intelligence, that her mother half doubted whether she were not acquainted with the secret spell of her existence, and might not now reveal herself.

"Yes; I am little Pearl!" repeated the child, continuing her antics.

"Thou art not my child! Thou art no Pearl of mine!" said the mother, half playfully; for it was often the case that a sportive impulse came over her, in the midst of her deepest suffering. "Tell me, then, what thou art, and who sent thee hither."

"Tell *me*, mother!" said the child, seriously, coming up to Hester, and pressing herself close to her knees. "Do thou tell *me!*"

"Thy Heavenly Father sent thee!" answered Hester Prynne.

But she said it with a hesitation that did not escape the child. Whether moved only by her ordinary freakishness, or because an evil spirit prompted her, she put up her small forefinger, and touched the scarlet letter.

"He did not send me! I have no Heavenly Father!" she cried.

"Hush, Pearl, hush! Thou must not talk so!" answered the mother, suppressing a groan. "He sent us all into this world. He sent even me, thy mother. Then, much more, thee! Or, if not, thou strange and elfish child, whence didst thou come?"

"Tell me! Tell me!" repeated Pearl, no longer seriously, but laughing, and capering about the floor. "It is thou that must tell *me!*"

7 *The Governor's Hall*

Hester Prynne went, one day, to the mansion of Governor Bellingham, with a pair of gloves, which she had embroidered to his order, and which were to be worn on some great occasion of state; for, though the chances of a popular election had caused this former ruler to descend a step or two from the highest rank, he still held an honorable and influential place among the colonial magistracy.

Another—and far more important—reason than the delivery of a pair of embroidered gloves impelled Hester, at this time, to seek an interview with a personage of so much power and activity in the affairs of the settlement. It had reached her ears that there was a design on the part of some of the leading inhabitants to deprive her of her child. On the supposition that Pearl was of demon origin, these good people not unreasonably argued that a Christian interest in the mother's soul required them to remove such a stumbling-block from her path. If the child, on the other hand, were really capable of moral and religious growth, and possessed the elements of ultimate salvation, then, surely, it would enjoy all the fairer prospect of these advantages by being transferred to wiser and better guardianship than Hester Prynne's. Among those who promoted the design, Governor Bellingham was said to be one of the most busy. It may appear singular, and indeed not a little absurd, that an affair of this kind, which, in later days, would have been referred to no higher authority than that of the selectmen of the town, should then have been a question publicly discussed, and on which statesmen of eminence took sides. At that epoch of primitive simplicity, however, matters of even slighter public interest, and of far less intrinsic weight, than the welfare of Hester and her child, were strangely mixed up with the deliberations of legislators and acts of state.

Full of concern, therefore,—but so conscious of her own right that it seemed scarcely an unequal match between the public, on the one side, and a lonely woman, backed by the sympathies of nature, on the other,—Hester Prynne set forth from her solitary cottage. Little Pearl, of course, was her companion. She was now of an age to run lightly along by her mother's side, and, constantly in motion, from morn till sunset, could have accomplished a much longer journey than that before her. Often, nevertheless, more from caprice[1] than necessity, she demanded to be taken up; but soon demanded to be set down again, and frisked onward before Hester on the grassy pathway, with many a harmless trip and tumble. We have spoken of Pearl's rich and luxuriant beauty; a beauty that shone with deep and vivid tints; a bright complexion, eyes possessing intensity both of depth and glow, and hair already of a deep, glossy brown, which, in after years, would be nearly akin to black. Her mother, in contriving the child's garb, had allowed the gorgeous tendencies of her imagination their full play; arraying her in a crimson velvet tunic, of a peculiar cut, abundantly embroidered with gold-thread. So much strength of coloring, which must have given a wan and pallid aspect to cheeks of a fainter bloom, was admirably adapted to Pearl's beauty, and made her the very brightest little jet of flame that ever danced upon the earth.

[1] caprice: sudden, odd change in behavior

But it was a remarkable attribute of this garb, and, indeed, of the child's whole appearance, that it reminded the beholder of the token which Hester Prynne was doomed to wear upon her bosom. It was the scarlet letter in another form; the scarlet letter endowed with life! The mother herself—as if the red blemish were so deeply scorched into her brain that all her conceptions assumed its form—had carefully wrought out the similitude; lavishing many hours of unhealthy ingenuity, to create a likeness between the object of her affection and the emblem of her guilt and torture. But, in truth, Pearl was the one, as well as the other; and only in consequence of that identity had Hester contrived so perfectly to represent the scarlet letter in her appearance.

As the two wayfarers came within the limits of the town, the children of the Puritans looked up from their play,—or what passed for play with those sombre little urchins,—and spoke gravely one to another:—

"Behold, verily, there is the woman of the scarlet letter; and, of a truth, moreover, there is the likeness of the scarlet letter running along by her side! Come, therefore, and let us fling mud at them!"

But Pearl, who was a dauntless child, after frowning, stamping her foot, and shaking her little hand with a variety of threatening gestures, suddenly made a rush at the knot of her enemies, and put them all to flight. She resembled, in her fierce pursuit, an infant pestilence whose mission was to punish the sins of the rising generation. She screamed and shouted, too, with a terrific volume of sound, which, doubtless, caused the hearts of the fugitives to quake. The victory won, Pearl returned quietly to her mother, and looked up, smiling into her face.

Without further adventure, they reached the dwelling of Governor Bellingham. This was a large wooden house, built in a fashion of which specimens still exist in the

streets of our older towns; now moss-grown, crumbling to decay, and melancholy at heart with many sorrowful or joyful occurrences, remembered or forgotten, that have happened, and passed away, within their dusky chambers. Then, however, there was the freshness of the passing year on its exterior, and the cheerfulness, gleaming forth from the sunny windows, of a human habitation, into which death had never entered. It had, indeed, a very cheery aspect; the walls being overspread with a kind of stucco, in which fragments of broken glass were plentifully inter-mixed; so that, when the sunshine fell aslant-wise over the front of the edifice, it glittered and sparkled as if dia-monds had been flung against it by the double handful. The brilliancy might have befitted Aladdin's palace,[2] rather than the mansion of a grave old Puritan ruler.

[2] Aladdin's palace: In the *Arabian Nights,* Aladdin discovers a magic lamp by means of which he builds a magnificent palace for his bride, the Sultan's daughter.

Pearl, looking at this bright wonder of a house, began to caper and dance, and imperatively demanded that the whole breadth of sunshine should be stripped off its front and given her to play with.

"No, my little Pearl!" said her mother. "Thou must gather thine own sunshine. I have none to give thee!"

They approached the door, which was of an arched form, and flanked on each side by a narrow tower or projection of the edifice, in both of which were lattice-windows, with wooden shutters to close over them at need. Lifting the iron hammer that hung at the portal, Hester Prynne gave a summons, which was answered by one of the Governor's bond servants, a free-born Englishman, but now a seven years' slave. During that term he was to be the property of his master, and as much a commodity of bargain and sale as an ox, or a joint-stool. The serf wore a blue coat, which was the customary garb of servingmen of that period, and long before, in the old hereditary halls of England.

"Is Governor Bellingham within?" inquired Hester.

"Yea, forsooth," replied the bond servant, staring with wide-open eyes at the scarlet letter, which, being a new-comer in the country, he had never before seen. "Yea, his honorable worship is within. But he hath a godly minister or two with him, and likewise a leech. Ye may not see his worship now."

"Nevertheless, I will enter," replied Hester Prynne, and the bond servant, perhaps judging from her manner, and the glittering symbol in her bosom, that she was a great lady offered no opposition.

So the mother and little Pearl were admitted into the hall of entrance. With many variations, suggested by the nature of his building-materials, diversity of climate, and a different mode of social life, Governor Bellingham had planned his new habitation after the residences of gentle-men of fair estate in his native land. Here, then, was a wide and reasonably lofty hall, extending through the whole depth of the house, and forming a medium of gen-eral communication, more or less directly, with all the other apartments. At one end, this spacious room was lighted by the windows of the two towers, which formed a small recess on either side of the portal. At the other end, though partly muffled by a curtain, it was more powerfully illu-minated by one of those embowed hall-windows which we read of in old books, and which was provided with a deep and cushioned seat. The furniture of the hall consisted of some ponderous chairs, the backs of which were elabo-rately carved with wreaths of oaken flowers; and likewise a table in the same taste; the whole being of the Elizabe-than age, or perhaps earlier, and heirlooms, transferred hither from the Governor's paternal home. On the table—in token that the sentiment of old English hospitality had not been left behind—stood a large pewter tankard, at the bottom of which, had Hester or Pearl peeped into it, they might have seen the frothy remnant of a recent draught of ale.

On the wall hung a row of portraits, representing the forefathers of the Bellingham line, some with armor on their breasts, and others with stately ruffs and robes of peace. All were characterized by the sternness and severity which old portraits always put on; as if they were the ghosts, rather than the pictures, of departed worthies, and were gazing with harsh and intolerant criticism at the pursuits and enjoyments of living men.

At about the centre of the oaken panels, that lined the hall, was suspended a suit of mail, not, like the pictures, an ancestral relic, but of the most modern date; for it had been manufactured by a skillful armorer in London, the same year—1634—in which Governor Bellingham came over to New England. There was a steel headpiece, pieces of armor for the body, throat, and legs, with a pair of iron gloves and a sword hanging beneath; all, and especially the helmet and breastplate, so highly burnished as to glow with white radiance, and scatter an illumination every-where about upon the floor. This bright equipment was not meant for mere idle show, but had been worn by the Governor on many a solemn training field, and had glit-tered, moreover, at the head of a regiment in the Pequod war.[3] For, though bred a lawyer, the emergencies of this new country had transformed Governor Bellingham into a soldier as well as a statesman and ruler.

Little Pearl—who was as greatly pleased with the gleaming armor as she had been with the glittering front of the house—spent some time looking into the polished mirror of the breastplate.

[3] Pequod war: the war against the Pequod Indians

"Mother," cried she, "I see you here. Look! Look!"

Hester looked, by way of humoring the child, and she saw that, owing to the peculiar effect of this convex mirror, the scarlet letter was represented in gigantic proportions, so as to be greatly the most prominent feature of her appearance. In truth, she seemed absolutely hidden behind it. Pearl pointed upward, also, at a similar picture in the headpiece; smiling at her mother, with the elfish intelligence that was so familiar an expression on her small face. That look of naughty merriment was likewise reflected in the mirror, with so much intensity that it made Hester Prynne feel as if it could not be the image of her own child, but of an imp who was seeking to mould itself into Pearl's shape.

"Come along, Pearl," said she, drawing her away. "Come and look into this fair garden. It may be we shall see flowers there; more beautiful ones than we find in the woods."

Pearl, accordingly, ran to the bow-window, at the farther end of the hall, and looked along the vista of a garden-walk, carpeted with closely shaven grass, and bordered with some rude attempt at shrubbery. But the proprietor appeared already to have given up, as hopeless, the effort to continue on this side of the Atlantic, in a hard soil and amid the close struggle for subsistence, the native English taste for ornamental gardening. Cabbages grew in plain sight; and a pumpkin-vine, rooted at some distance, had run across the intervening space, and deposited one of its gigantic products directly beneath the hall-window; as if to warn the Governor that this great lump of vegetable gold was as rich an ornament as New England earth would offer him. There were a few rosebushes, however, and a number of apple-trees.

Pearl, seeing the rosebushes, began to cry for a red rose, and would not be pacified.

"Hush, child, hush!" said her mother, earnestly. "Do not cry, dear little Pearl! I hear voices in the garden. The Governor is coming, and gentlemen with him!"

In fact, down the vista of the garden avenue a number of persons were seen approaching the house. Pearl, in utter scorn of her mother's attempt to quiet her, gave an uncanny scream, and then became silent; not from any notion of obedience, but because the quick curiosity of her disposition was excited by the appearance of these new personages.

The Elf-Child and the Minister

Governor Bellingham, in a loose gown and easy cap, walked foremost, and appeared to be showing off his estate, and talking at great length on his projected improvements. The wide circumference of an elaborate ruff, beneath his gray beard, in the antiquated fashion of King James's reign, caused his head to look not a little like that of John the Baptist on a platter. The impression made by his aspect, so rigid and severe, and frost-bitten with more than autumnal age, was hardly in keeping with the appliances of worldly enjoyment wherewith he had evidently done his utmost to surround himself. But it is an error to suppose that our grave forefathers—though accustomed to speak and think of human existence as a state merely of trial and warfare, and though prepared to sacrifice goods and life at the behest[1] of duty—made it a matter of conscience to reject such means of comfort, or even luxury, as lay fairly within their grasp. This creed was never taught, for instance, by the venerable pastor, John Wilson, whose beard, white as a snowdrift, was seen over Governor Bellingham's shoulder; while its wearer suggested that pears and peaches might yet be naturalized in the New England climate, and that purple grapes might be compelled to

[1] behest: bidding

70

flourish, against the sunny garden-wall. The old clergyman, nurtured at the rich bosom of the English Church, had a long-established and legitimate taste for all good and comfortable things; and however stern he might show himself in the pulpit, or in his public reproof of such transgressions as that of Hester Prynne, still, the genial benevolence of his private life had won him warmer affection than was accorded any of his professional contemporaries.

Behind the Governor and Mr. Wilson came two other guests; the Reverend Arthur Dimmesdale, whom the reader may remember as having taken a brief and reluctant part in the scene of Hester Prynne's disgrace; and, in close companionship with him, old Roger Chillingworth, a person of great skill in physic, who, for two or three years past, had been settled in the town. It was understood that this learned man was the physician as well as friend of the young minister, whose health had severely suffered, of late, because of his too conscientious attention to his duties.

The Governor, in advance of his visitors, ascended one or two steps, and, throwing open the leaves of the great hall-window, found himself close to little Pearl. The shadow of the curtain fell on Hester Prynne, and partially concealed her.

"What have we here?" said Governor Bellingham, looking with surprise at the scarlet little figure before him. "I profess, I have never seen the like, since my days of vanity, in old King James's time, when I was wont to esteem it a high favor to be admitted to a court mask!² But how got such a guest into my hall?"

"Ay, indeed!" cried good old Mr. Wilson. "What little bird of scarlet plumage may this be? Methinks I have seen just such figures when the sun has been shining through a richly painted window, and tracing out the golden and crimson images across the floor. But that was in the old

² mask: a dramatic entertainment

land. Prithee, young one, who art thou, and what has ailed thy mother to dress thee in this strange fashion? Art thou a Christian child? Dost know thy catechism? Or art thou one of those naughty elfs or fairies, whom we thought to have left behind us, with other relics of Papistry, in merry Old England?"

"I am mother's child," answered the scarlet vision, "and my name is Pearl!"

"Pearl?—Ruby, rather!—or Coral!—or Red Rose, at the very least, judging from thy hue!" responded the old minister, putting forth his hand in a vain attempt to pat little Pearl on the cheek. "But where is this mother of thine? Ah! I see," he added; and turning to Governor Bellingham, whispered, "This is the child of whom we have held speech together; and behold here the unhappy woman, Hester Prynne, her mother!"

"Sayest thou so?" cried the Governor. "But she comes at a good time; and we will look into this matter forthwith."

Governor Bellingham stepped through the window into the hall, followed by his three guests.

"Hester Prynne," said he, "there hath been much question concerning thee, of late. The point hath been weightily discussed, whether we, that are of authority and influence, do well discharge our consciences by trusting an immortal soul, such as there is in yonder child, to the guidance of one who hath stumbled and fallen, amid the pitfalls of this world. Speak thou, the child's own mother! Were it not, thinkest thou, for thy little one's temporal and eternal welfare that she be taken out of thy charge, and clad soberly, and disciplined strictly, and instructed in the truths of heaven and earth? What canst thou do for the child, in this kind?"

"I can teach my little Pearl what I have learned from this!" answered Hester Prynne, laying her finger on the red token.

"Woman, it is thy badge of shame!" replied the stern magistrate. "It is because of the stain which that letter indicates, that we would transfer thy child to other hands."

"Nevertheless," said the mother, calmly, though growing pale, "this badge hath taught me—it daily teaches me—it is teaching me at this moment—lessons whereof my child may be the wiser and better albeit they can profit nothing to myself."

"We will judge warily," said Bellingham, "and look well what we are about to do. Good Master Wilson, I pray you, examine this Pearl,—since that is her name,—and see whether she hath had such Christian teaching as befits a child of her age."

The old minister seated himself in an armchair, and made an effort to draw Pearl betwixt his knees. But the child, unaccustomed to the touch of familiarity of any but her mother, escaped through the open window, and stood on the upper step looking like a wild tropical bird, of rich plumage, ready to take flight into the upper air. Mr. Wilson, not a little astonished at this outbreak,—for he was a grandfatherly sort of person, and usually a vast favorite with children,—tried, however, to proceed with the examination.

"Pearl," said he, with great solemnity, "thou must take heed to instruction, that so, in due season, thou mayest wear in thy bosom the pearl of great price. Canst thou tell me, my child, who made thee?"

Now Pearl knew well enough who made her; for Hester Prynne, the daughter of a pious home, very soon after her talk with the child about her Heavenly Father, had begun to inform her of those truths which the human spirit, at whatever stage of immaturity, imbibes with such eager interest. Pearl, therefore, so large were the attainments of her three years' lifetime, could have borne a fair examination in the New England Primer, or in the first column of the Westminster Catechisms, although unacquainted with the outward form of those celebrated works. But that perversity[3] which all children have more or less of, and of which little Pearl had a tenfold portion, now, at the most inopportune moment, took thorough possession of her, and closed her lips, or impelled her to speak words amiss. After putting her finger in her mouth, with many ungracious refusals to answer good Mr. Wilson's questions, the child finally announced that she had not been made at all, but had been plucked by her mother off the bush of wild roses that grew by the prison-door.

This fantasy was probably suggested by the near proximity of the Governor's red roses, as Pearl stood outside of the window; together with her recollection of the prison rosebush, which she had passed in coming hither.

Old Roger Chillingworth, with a smile on his face, whispered something in the young clergyman's ear. Hester Prynne looked at the man of skill, and even then, with her fate hanging in the balance, was started to perceive what a change had come over his features,—how much uglier they were,—how his dark complexion seemed to have grown duskier, and his figure more misshapen,—since the days when she had known him. She met his eyes for an instant, but was immediately constrained to give all her attention to the scene now going forward.

"This is awful!" cried the Governor, slowly recovering from the astonishment into which Pearl's response had thrown him. "Here is a child of three years old, and she cannot tell who made her! Without question, she is equally in the dark as to her soul, its present depravity, and future destiny! Methinks, gentlemen, we need inquire no further."

Hester caught hold of Pearl, and drew her forcibly into her arms, confronting the old Puritan magistrate with

3 perversity: willfulness

almost a fierce expression. Alone in the world, cast off by it, and with this sole treasure to keep her heart alive, she felt that she possessed sacred rights against the world, and was ready to defend them to the death.

"God gave me the child!" cried she. "He gave her in requital of all things else, which ye had taken from me. She is my happiness!—she is my torture, none the less! Pearl keeps me here in life! Pearl punishes me too! See ye not, she is the scarlet letter, only capable of being loved, and so endowed with a million-fold the power of retribution for my sin? Ye shall not take her! I will die first!"

"My poor woman," said the not unkind old minister, "the child shall be well cared for!—far better than thou canst do it."

"God gave her into my keeping," repeated Hester Prynne, raising her voice almost to a shriek. "I *will not* give her up!"—And here, by a sudden impulse, she turned to the young clergyman, at whom, up to this moment, she had seemed hardly so much as once to direct her eyes.— "Speak thou for me!" cried she. "Thou wast my pastor, and hadst charge of my soul, and knowest me better than these men can. I will not lose the child! Speak for me! Thou knowest,—for thou hast sympathies which these men lack!—thou knowest what is in my heart, and what are a mother's rights, and how much stronger they are, when that mother has but her child and the scarlet letter! Look thou to it! I will not lose the child! Look to it!"

At this wild appeal, which indicated that Hester Prynne's situation had provoked her to little less than madness, the young minister at once came forward, pale, and holding his hand over his heart, as was his custom whenever his peculiarly nervous temperament was disturbed. He looked now more careworn and emaciated than as we described him at the scene of Hester's public ignomity; and whether it were his failing health, or whatever the cause, his large dark eyes had a world of pain in their troubled and melancholy depth.

"There is truth in what she says," began the minister, "truth in what Hester says, and in the feeling which inspires her! God gave her the child, and gave her, too, an instinctive knowledge of its nature and requirements,— both seemingly so peculiar,—which no other mortal being can possess. And, moreover, is there not a quality of awful sacredness in the relation between this mother and child?"

"Ay!—how is that, good Master Dimmesdale?" interrupted the Governor. "Make that plain, I pray you!"

"It must be even so," resumed the minister. "For, if we deem it otherwise, do we not thereby say that the Heavenly Father, the Creator of all flesh, hath lightly recognized a deed of sin, and made of no account the distinction between unhallowed lust and holy love? This child of its father's guilt and its mother's shame hath come from the hand of God, to work in many ways upon her heart, who pleads so earnestly, and with such bitterness of spirit, the right to keep her. It was meant for a blessing, for the one blessing of her life! It was meant, doubtless, as the mother herself hath told us, for a retribution too; a torture to be felt at many an unthought-of moment; a pang, a sting, a constant agony, in the midst of a troubled joy! Hath she not expressed this thought in the garb of the poor child, so forcibly reminding us of that red symbol which sears her bosom?"

"Well said again!" cried Mr. Wilson. "I feared the woman had no better thought than to make a public display!"

"Oh, not so!—not so!" continued Mr. Dimmesdale. "She recognizes, believe me, the solemn miracle which God hath wrought, in the existence of that child. And may she feel, too,—what, methinks, is the very truth,—that this boon was meant, above all things else, to keep the mother's soul alive, and to preserve her from blacker depths of sin into which Satan might else have sought to plunge her! Therefore it is good for this poor, sinful woman that she hath an infant, a being capable of eternal joy or sorrow, confided to her care,—to be trained up by her to right-eousness,—to remind her, at every moment, of her fall,—but yet to teach her, as it were by the Creator's sacred pledge, that, if she bring the child to heaven, the child also will bring her thither! Herein is the sinful mother happier than the sinful father. For Hester Prynne's sake, then, and no less for the poor child's sake, let us leave them as Providence hath seen fit to place them!"

"You speak, my friend, with a strange earnestness," said old Roger Chillingworth, smiling at him.

"And there is much weight in what my young brother hath spoken," added the Reverend Mr. Wilson. "What say you, Master Bellingham? Has he not pleaded well?"

"Indeed he has," answered the magistrate, "and has offered such arguments, that we will even leave the matter as it now stands; so long, at least, as there shall be no further scandal in the woman. Care must be had, never-theless, to put the child to regular examination in the catechism, at thy hands or Master Dimmesdale's. More-over, at a proper season, the tithing-men[4] must take heed that she go both to school and to church."

The young minister, on ceasing to speak, had with-drawn a few steps from the group, and stood with his face partially concealed in the heavy folds of the window-cur-tains; while the shadow of his figure, which the sunlight cast upon the floor, was trembling with the strength of his appeal. Pearl, that wild and flighty little elf, stole softly towards him, and taking his hand in the grasp of both her own, laid her cheek against it; a caress so tender, and withal so unobtrusive, that her mother, who was looking

[4] tithing-men: officers in the New England colonies who saw to it that Sunday was religiously observed

on, asked herself,—"Is that my Pearl?" Yet she knew that there was love in the child's heart, although it mostly revealed itself in passion, and hardly twice in her lifetime had been softened by such gentleness as now. The minister looked round, laid his hand on the child's head, hesitated an instant, and then kissed her brow. Little Pearl's unusual mood of sentiment lasted no longer; she laughed, and went capering down the hall, so airily, that old Mr. Wilson raised a question whether even her tiptoes touched the floor.

"The little baggage hath witchcraft in her, I profess," said he to Dimmesdale. "She needs no old woman's broomstick to fly withal!"

"A strange child!" remarked old Roger Chillingworth. "It is easy to see the mother's part in her. Would it be beyond a philosopher's skill, think ye, gentlemen, to analyze the child's nature, and, from its make and mould, to give a shrewd guess at the father?"

"Nay; it would be sinful, in such a question, to follow the clew of profane philosophy," said Mr. Wilson. "Better to fast and pray upon it; and still better to leave the mystery as we find it, unless Providence reveal it of its own accord. Thereby, every good Christian man hath a title to show a father's kindness towards the poor, deserted babe."

The affair being so satisfactorily concluded, Hester Prynne, with Pearl, left the house. As they descended the steps, it is declared that the lattice of a chamber-window was thrown open, and forth into the sunny day was thrust the face of Mistress Hibbins, Governor Bellingham's bitter-tempered sister, who, a few years later, was executed as a witch.

"Hist, hist!" said she, while her ugly face seemed to cast a shadow over the cheerful newness of the house. "Wilt thou go with us to-night? There will be a merry company in the forest; and I well-nigh promised the Black Man that comely Hester Prynne should make one."

"Make my excuse to him, so please you!" answered Hester, with a triumphant smile. "I must tarry at home, and keep watch over my little Pearl. Had they taken her from me, I would willingly have gone with thee into the forest, and signed my name in the Black Man's book too, and that with mine own blood!"

"We shall have thee there anon!" said the witch-lady, frowning, as she drew back her head.

But here—if we suppose this interview betwixt Mistress Hibbins and Hester Prynne to be authentic, and not a parable—was already an illustration of the young minister's argument against sundering the relation of a fallen mother to the offspring of her frailty. Even thus early had the child saved her from Satan's snare.

9   *The Leech*[1]

Under the appellation of Roger Chillingworth, the reader will remember, was hidden another name, which its former wearer had resolved should never more be spoken. It has been related how, in the crowd that witnessed Hester Prynne's ignominious exposure, stood a man, elderly, travel-worn, who, just emerging from the perilous wilderness, beheld the woman, in whom he hoped to find embodied the warmth and cheerfulness of home, set up as a type of sin before the people. Her matronly frame was trodden under all men's feet. Infamy was babbling around her in the public market place. For her kindred, should the tidings ever reach them, and for the companions of her unspotted life, there remained nothing but the contagion of her dishonor,—which would not fail to be distributed in strict accordance and proportion with the intimacy and sacredness of their previous relationship. Then why—since the choice was with himself—should the individual, whose connection with the fallen woman had been the most intimate and sacred of them all, come forward to vindicate his claim to an inheritance so little desirable? He resolved not to be pilloried beside her on her pedestal of shame. Unknown to all but Hester Prynne, and possessing

[1] leech: an old word for physician, from the name of a bloodsucking worm formerly used by doctors to draw blood from patients

the lock and key of her silence, he chose to withdraw his name from the roll of mankind, and, as regarded his former ties and interests, to vanish out of life as completely as if he indeed lay at the bottom of the ocean, whither rumor had long ago consigned him. This purpose once effected, new interests would immediately spring up, and likewise a new purpose; dark, it is true, if not guilty, but of force enough to engage the full strength of his faculties.

In pursuance of this resolve, he took up his residence in the Puritan town as Roger Chillingworth, without other introduction than the learning and intelligence of which he possessed more than a common measure. As his studies, at a previous period of his life, had made him fully acquainted with medical science, it was as a physician that he now presented himself, and as such was cordially received. Skillful men, of the medical and surgical profession, were of rare occurrence in the colony. They seldom, it would appear, partook of [2] the religious zeal that brought other emigrants across the Atlantic. In their researches into the human frame, it may be that the higher and more subtle faculties of such men were materialized, and that they lost the spiritual view of existence amid the intricacies of that wondrous mechanism, which seemed to involve art enough to comprise all of life within itself. At all events, the health of the good town of Boston, so far as medicine had aught to do with it, had hitherto lain in the guardianship of an aged deacon[3] and druggist, whose piety and godly deportment were stronger testimonials in his favor than any that he could have produced in the shape of a diploma. The only surgeon was one who combined the occasional exercise of that noble art with the daily and habitual flourish of a razor. To such a professional body Roger Chillingworth was a brilliant acquisition. He soon

[2] partook of: shared

[3] deacon: a layman who assists the pastor of a church in various ways

manifested his familiarity with the ponderous and impos-
ing machinery of antique physic. In his Indian captivity,
moreover, he had gained much knowledge of the properties
of native herbs and roots; nor did he conceal from his
patients, that these simple medicines, Nature's boon to the
untutored savage, had quite as large a share of his own
confidence as the European drugs, which so many learned
doctors had spent centuries in elaborating.

This learned stranger was exemplary, as regarded, at
least, the outward forms of a religious life, and, soon after
his arrival, had chosen for his spiritual guide the Reverend
Mr. Dimmesdale. The young divine, whose scholar-like
renown still lived in Oxford, was considered by his more
fervent admirers as little less than a heaven-ordained apostle, destined, should he live and labor for the ordinary term
of life, to do as great deeds for the now feeble New England
Church as the early Fathers had achieved for the infancy
of the Christian faith. About this period, however, his
health had evidently begun to fail. By those best acquainted with his habits, the paleness of the young minister's cheek was accounted for by his too earnest devotion
to study, his scrupulous fulfilment of parochial duty, and,
more than all, by the fasts and vigils of which he made a
frequent practice, in order to keep the grossness of this
earthly state from clogging and obscuring his spiritual
lamp. Some declared, that, if he were really going to die,
it was cause enough, that the world was not worthy to be
any longer trodden by his feet. He himself, on the other
hand, with characteristic humility, avowed his belief, that,
if Providence should see fit to remove him, it would be
because of his own unworthiness to perform its humblest
mission here on earth. With all this difference of opinion
as to the cause of his decline, there could be no question
of the fact. His form grew emaciated; his voice, though
still rich and sweet, had a certain melancholy prophecy of

decay in it; he was often observed, on any slight alarm or other sudden accident, to put his hand over his heart, with first a flush and then a paleness, indicative of pain.

Such was the young clergyman's condition, and so near the prospect that his dawning light would be extinguished, all untimely, when Roger Chillingworth made his appearance in the town. His first entry on the scene, few people could tell whence, dropping down, as it were, out of the sky, or starting from the lower earth, had an aspect of mystery, which was easily heightened to the miraculous. He was now known to be a man of skill; it was observed that he gathered herbs, and the blossoms of wild flowers, and dug up roots, and plucked off twigs from the forest-trees, like one acquainted with hidden virtues in what was valueless to common eyes. He was heard to speak of Sir Kenelm Digby,[4] and other famous men,—whose scientific attainments were esteemed hardly less than supernatural,—as having been his correspondents or associates. Why, with such rank in the learned world, had he come hither? What could he, whose sphere was in great cities, be seeking in the wilderness? In answer to this query, a rumor gained ground,—and, however absurd, was entertained by some very sensible people,—that Heaven had wrought an absolute miracle, by transporting an eminent Doctor of Medicine, from a German university, bodily through the air, and setting him down at the door of Dimmesdale's study!

The idea was supported by the strong interest which the physician ever manifested in the young clergyman; he attached himself to him as a parishioner, and sought to win a friendly regard and confidence from his naturally reserved sensibility. He expressed great alarm at his pastor's state of health, but was anxious to attempt the cure, and, if early undertaken, seemed not despondent of a

[4] Digby: English scientist (1603–1665)

favorable result. The elders, the deacons, the motherly dames, and the young and fair maidens, of Dimmesdale's flock, were alike anxious that he should make trial of the physician's frankly offered skill. Dimmesdale gently repelled their entreaties.

"I need no medicine," said he.

But how could the young minister say so, when, with every successive Sabbath, his cheek was paler and thinner, and his voice more tremulous than before,—when it had now become a constant habit, rather than a casual gesture, to press his hand over his heart? Was he weary of his labors? Did he wish to die? These questions were solemnly propounded to him by the elder ministers of Boston and the deacons of his church, who, to use their own phrase, "dealt with him" on the sin of rejecting the aid which Providence so manifestly held out. He listened in silence, and finally promised to confer with the physician.

"Were it God's will," said Dimmesdale, when, in fulfilment of this pledge, he requested old Roger Chillingworth's professional advice, "I could be well content that my labors, and my sorrows, and my sins, and my pains, should shortly end with me, and what is earthly of them be buried in my grave, and the spiritual go with me to my eternal state, rather than that you should put your skill to the proof in my behalf."

"Ah," replied Roger Chillingworth, "it is thus that a young clergyman is apt to speak. Youthful men, not having taken a deep root, give up their hold of life so easily! And saintly men, who walk with God on earth, would fain be away, to walk with him on the golden pavements of the New Jerusalem."

"Nay," rejoined the young minister, putting his hand to his heart, with a flush of pain flitting over his brow, "were I worthier to walk there, I could be better content to toil here."

"Good men ever interpret themselves too meanly,"[5] said the physician.

In this manner, the mysterious old Roger Chillingworth became the medical adviser of the Reverend Mr. Dimmesdale. As not only the disease interested the physician, but he was strongly moved to look into the character and qualities of the patient, these two men, so different in age, came gradually to spend much time together. For the sake of the minister's health, and to enable the doctor to gather plants with healing balm in them, they took long walks on the seashore, or in the forest; mingling various talk with the murmur of the waves, and the solemn wind-anthem among the treetops. Often, likewise, one was the guest of the other, in his place of study and retirement. There was a fascination for the minister in the company of the man of science, in whom he recognized an intellectual cultivation of no moderate depth or scope; together with a range and freedom of ideas that he would have vainly looked for among the members of his own profession. In truth, he was startled, if not shocked, to find this attribute in the physician. Dimmesdale was a true priest, with the reverential sentiment largely developed, and an order of mind that impelled itself powerfully along the track of a creed, and wore its passage continually deeper with the lapse of time. In no state of society would he have been what is called a man of liberal views; it would always be essential to his peace to feel the pressure of a faith about him, supporting, while it confined him within its iron framework. Not the less, however, though with a tremulous enjoyment, did he feel the occasional relief of looking at the universe through the medium of another kind of intellect than those with which he habitually held converse.

Thus Roger Chillingworth scrutinized his patient

5 meanly: humbly

carefully, both as he saw him in his ordinary life, and as he appeared when thrown amidst other moral scenery, the novelty of which might call out something new to the surface of his character. He deemed it essential, it would seem, to know the man, before attempting to do him good. Wherever there is a heart and an intellect, the diseases of the physical frame are tinged with the peculiarities of these. In Arthur Dimmesdale, thought and imagination were so active, and sensibility so intense, that the bodily infirmity would be likely to have its groundwork there. So Roger Chillingworth—the man of skill, the kind and friendly physician—strove to go deep into his patient's bosom, delving among his principles, prying into his recollections, and probing everything with a cautious touch, like a treasure-seeker in a dark cavern. Few secrets can escape an investigator, who has opportunity and license to undertake such a quest, and skill to follow it up. A man burdened with a secret should especially avoid the intimacy of his physician. If the latter possess native sagacity,[6] and a nameless something more, if he have the power, which must be born with him, to bring his mind into such affinity with his patient's, that this last shall unawares have spoken what he imagines himself only to have thought; if such revelations be received without tumult, and acknowledged not so often by an uttered sympathy as by silence, an inarticulate breath, and here and there a word, to indicate that all is understood; if to these qualifications of a confidant be joined the advantages afforded by his unrecognized character as a physician,—then, at some inevitable moment, will the soul of the sufferer be dissolved, and flow forth in a dark but transparent stream, bringing all its mysteries into the daylight.

Roger Chillingworth possessed all, or most, of the attributes above enumerated. Nevertheless, time went on; a

[6] sagacity: shrewdness

kind of intimacy grew up between these two cultivated minds, which had a wide field to meet upon; they discussed every topic of ethics and religion, of public affairs and private character; they talked much, on both sides, of matters that seemed personal to themselves; and yet no secret, such as the physician fancied must exist there, ever stole out of the minister's consciousness into his companion's ear.

After a time, at a hint from Roger Chillingworth, the friends of Dimmesdale effected an arrangement by which the two were lodged in the same house; so that every ebb and flow of the minister's life-tide might pass under the eye of his anxious and attached physician. There was much joy throughout the town when this highly desirable object was attained. It was held to be the best possible measure for the young clergyman's welfare; unless, indeed, as often urged by such as felt authorized to do so, he had selected some one of the many blooming damsels, spiritually devoted to him, to become his devoted wife. This latter step, however, there was no present prospect that Arthur Dimmesdale would be prevailed upon to take; he rejected all suggestions of the kind, as if priestly celibacy[7] were one of his articles of church-discipline. Doomed by his own choice, therefore, as he so evidently was, to eat his unsavory morsel always at another's board, and endure the lifelong chill which must be his lot who seeks to warm himself only at another's fireside, it truly seemed that this sagacious, experienced, benevolent old physician was the very man of all men to be constantly within reach of his voice.

The new abode of the two friends was with a pious widow, of good social rank, who dwelt in a house covering pretty nearly the site on which the venerable structure of

---

[7] as if priestly celibacy, etc.: The state of being unmarried is required of Catholic priests; it does not apply to ministers like Dimmesdale.

King's Chapel has since been built. It had the graveyard,
originally Isaac Johnson's home-field, on one side, and so
well adapted to call up serious reflections, suited to their
respective employments, in both minister and doctor. The
motherly care of the good widow assigned to Mr. Dimmesdale a front apartment, with a sunny exposure, and heavy
window-curtains, to create a noontide shadow, when desirable. On the other side of the house, old Roger Chillingworth arranged his study and laboratory; not such as a
modern man of science would reckon even tolerably complete, but provided with a distilling apparatus, and the
means of compounding drugs and chemicals, which he
knew well how to use. With such commodiousness[8] of
situation, these two learned persons sat themselves down,
each in his own domain, yet familiarly passing from one
apartment to the other, and bestowing a mutual inspection
into one another's business.

And the Reverend Arthur Dimmesdale's best discerning friends, as we have intimated, very reasonably imagined that the hand of Providence had done all this, for the
purpose—besought in so many public, and domestic, and
secret prayers—of restoring the young minister to health.
But—it must now be said—another portion of the community had latterly begun to take its own view of the
relation betwixt the clergyman and the mysterious old physician. The people, in the case of which we speak, could
justify its prejudice against Roger Chillingworth by no fact
or argument worthy of serious refutation. There was an
aged handicraftsman, it is true, who had been a citizen of
London at the period of Sir Thomas Overbury's[9] murder,
now some thirty years ago; he testified to having seen the
physician, under some other name, which the narrator of

8 commodiousness: convenience
9 Sir Thomas Overbury: English writer (1581–1613)

the story had now forgotten, in company with Doctor Forman,[10] the famous old conjurer, who was implicated in the
affair of Overbury. Two or three individuals hinted that the
man of skill, during his Indian captivity, had enlarged his
medical skill by joining in the incantations of the savage
priests; who were universally acknowledged to be powerful

---

[10] Forman: Simon Forman, English astrologer (1552–1611)

enchanters, often performing seemingly miraculous cures by their skill in the black art. A large number—and many of these persons of such sober sense and practical observation that their opinions would have been valuable in other matters—affirmed that Roger Chillingworth's aspect had undergone a remarkable change while he had dwelt in town, and especially since his abode with Dimmesdale. At first his expression had been calm, meditative, and scholarlike. Now, there was something ugly and evil in his face, which they had not previously noticed, and which grew still more obvious to sight the oftener they looked upon him. According to the vulgar idea, the fire in his laboratory had been brought from the lower regions, and was fed with infernal fuel; and so, as might be expected, his visage was getting sooty with the smoke.

To sum up the matter, it grew to be a widely spread opinion that Arthur Dimmesdale, like many other personages of special sanctity, in all ages of the Christian world, was haunted either by Satan himself, or by Satan's agent, in the guise of old Roger Chillingworth. This diabolical agent had the Divine permission, for a season, to dig into the clergyman's intimacy, and plot against his soul. No sensible man, it was confessed, could doubt on which side the victory would turn. The people looked, with an unshaken hope, to see the minister come forth out of the conflict transfigured with the glory which he would unquestionably win. Meanwhile, nevertheless, it was sad to think of the mortal agony through which he must struggle towards his triumph.

Alas! to judge from the gloom and terror in the depths of the poor minister's eyes, the battle was a sore one, and the victory anything but secure.

10 *The Leech and His Patient*

Old Roger Chillingworth, all his life, had been calm in temperament, kindly, though not of warm affections, but ever, and in all his relations with the world, pure and upright. He had begun an investigation, as he imagined, with the severe honesty of a judge, desirous only of truth, as if the question involved no more than a geometrical problem, instead of human passions, and wrongs inflicted on himself. But, as he proceeded, a terrible fascination, a kind of fierce, though still calm, necessity seized him, and never set him free again. He now dug into the poor clergyman's heart, like a miner searching for gold; or rather, like a sexton delving into a grave, possibly in quest of a jewel that had been buried on the dead man's bosom, but likely to find nothing save mortality and corruption. Alas for his own soul, if these were what he sought!

Sometimes a light glimmered out of the physician's eyes, burning blue and ominous like the reflection of a furnace, or, let us say, like one of those gleams of ghastly fire that darted from Bunyan's[1] awful doorway in the hillside, and quivered on the pilgrim's face. The soil where this dark miner was working had perchance shown indications that encouraged him.

"This man," said he, at such a moment, to himself,

[1] Bunyan: John Bunyan (1628–1688), English author of *Pilgrim's Progress*

"pure as they deem him,—all spiritual as he *seems*,—hath inherited a strong animal nature from his father or his mother. Let us dig further in the direction of this vein!"

Then, after long search into the minister's dim interior, and turning over many precious materials, he would turn back discouraged, and begin his quest towards another point. He groped along as stealthily, with as cautious a tread, and as wary an outlook, as a thief entering a chamber where a man lies only half asleep,—or, it may be, broad awake,—with purpose to steal the very treasure which this man guards as the apple of his eye. In spite of his premeditated carefulness, the floor would now and then creak; his garments would rustle; the shadow of his presence, in a forbidden proximity, would be thrown across his victim. In other words, Dimmesdale, whose sensibility of nerve often produced the effect of spiritual intuition, would become vaguely aware that something harmful to his peace had thrust itself into relation with him. But old Roger Chillingworth, too, had perceptions that were almost intuitive; and when the minister threw his startled eyes toward him, there the physician sat; his kind, watchful, sympathizing, but never intrusive friend.

Yet Dimmesdale would perhaps have seen this individual's character more perfectly, if a certain morbidness, to which sick hearts are liable, had not made him suspicious of all mankind. Trusting no man as his friend, he could not recognize his enemy when he actually appeared. He therefore still kept up a familiar friendship with him, daily receiving the old physician in his study; or visiting his laboratory, and, for recreation's sake, watching the process by which weeds were converted into powerful drugs.

One day, leaning his forehead on his hand, and his elbow on the sill of the open window, that looked towards the graveyard, he talked with Roger Chillingworth, while the old man was examining a bundle of plants.

"Where," asked he, looking askance at them,—for it was the clergyman's peculiarity that he seldom, nowadays, looked straight at any object, human or inanimate,—"Where, my kind doctor, did you gather those herbs, with such a dark, flabby leaf?"

"Even in the graveyard here at hand," answered the physician continuing his employment. "They are new to me. I found them growing on a grave, which bore no tombstone, nor other memorial of the dead man, save these ugly weeds, that have taken upon themselves to keep him in remembrance. They grew out of his heart, and typify, it may be, some hideous secret that was buried with him, and which he had done better to confess during his lifetime."

"Perchance,"[2] said Dimmesdale, "he earnestly desired it, but could not."

"And wherefore?" answered the physician. "Wherefore not; since all the powers of nature call so earnestly for the confession of sin, that these black weeds have sprung up out of a buried heart, to make manifest an unspoken crime?"

"That, good Sir, is but a fantasy of yours," replied the minister. "There can be, if I forebode aright, no power, short of the Divine mercy, to disclose, whether by uttered words, or by type or emblem, the secrets that may be buried in a human heart. The heart, making itself guilty of such secrets, must perforce hold them, until Judgment Day—when all hidden things shall be revealed. Nor have I so read or interpreted the Bible, as to understand that the disclosure of human thoughts and deeds, then to be made, is intended as a part of the retribution. That, surely, were a shallow view of it. No; these revelations, unless I greatly err, are meant merely to promote the intellectual satisfaction of all intelligent beings, who will stand waiting, on

[2] perchance: perhaps

that day, to see the dark problem of this life made plain. A knowledge of men's hearts will be needful to the fullest solution of that problem. And I conceive that hearts holding such miserable secrets will yield them up, at that last day, not with reluctance, but with joy unutterable."

"Then why not reveal them here?" asked Roger Chillingworth, glancing quietly at the minister. "Why should not the guilty ones sooner avail themselves of this *unutterable* solace?"

"They mostly do," said the clergyman, griping[3] hard at his breast as if afflicted with a throb of pain. "Many a poor soul hath given its confidence to me, not only on the death-bed, but while strong in life, and honest in reputation. And ever, after such an outpouring, oh, what a relief have I witnessed in those sinful brethren! even as in one who at last draws free air, after long stifling with his own polluted breath. How can it be otherwise? Why should a wretched man, guilty, we will say, of murder, prefer to keep the dead corpse buried in his own heart, rather than fling it forth at once, and let the universe take care of it!"

"Yet some men bury their secrets thus," observed the calm physician.

"True; there are such men," answered Dimmesdale. "But, not to suggest more obvious reasons, it may be that they are kept silent by the very constitution of their nature. Or, guilty as they may be, retaining, nevertheless, a zeal for God's glory and man's welfare, they shrink from displaying themselves black and filthy in the view of men; because, thenceforward, no good can be achieved by them; no evil of the past be redeemed by better service. So, to their own unutterable torment, they go about among their fellow-creatures, looking pure as new-fallen snow while their hearts are all spotted with iniquity of which they cannot rid themselves."

[3] griping: grasping

"These men deceive themselves," said Roger Chilling-worth, with emphasis, and making a slight gesture with his forefinger. "They fear to take up the shame that right-fully belongs to them. Their love for man, their zeal for God's service,—these holy impulses may or may not exist at the same time in their hearts with the evil inmates to which their guilt has unbarred the door, and which must needs propagate a hellish breed within them. But, if they seek to glorify God, let them not lift heavenward their unclean hands! If they would serve their fellowmen, let them do it by showing the power and reality of conscience, in constraining them to penitential self-abasement! Wouldst thou have me to believe, O wise and pious friend, that a false show can be better—can be more for God's glory, or man's welfare—than God's own truth? Believe me, such men deceive themselves!"

"It may be so," said the young clergyman, indifferently, as waiving a discussion that he considered irrelevant or unreasonable. "But, now, I would ask of my well-skilled physician whether he deems me to have profited by his kindly care of this weak frame of mine?"

Before Roger Chillingworth could answer, they heard the clear, wild laughter of a young child's voice, proceeding from the adjacent burial-ground. Looking instinctively from the open window,—for it was summertime,—the min-ister beheld Hester Prynne and little Pearl passing along the footpath that traversed the enclosure. Pearl, looking as beautiful as the day, was in one of those moods of perverse merriment which, whenever they occurred, seemed to re-move her entirely out of the sphere of sympathy or human contact. She now skipped irreverently from one grave to another; until, coming to the broad, flat, armorial tomb-stone of a departed worthy,—perhaps of Isaac Johnson himself,—she began to dance upon it. In reply to her moth-er's request that she would behave, little Pearl paused to gather the prickly burrs from a tall burdock which grew beside the tomb. Taking a handful of these, she arranged them along the lines of the scarlet letter that decorated the maternal bosom, to which the burrs, as their nature was, tenaciously adhered. Hester did not pluck them off.

Roger Chillingworth had by this time approached the window, and smiled grimly down.

"There is no law, nor reverence for authority, no regard for human ordinances or opinions, right or wrong, in that child's composition," remarked he, as much to himself as to his companion. "I saw her, the other day, bespatter the Governor himself with water, at the cattle-trough in Spring Lane. What, in Heaven's name, is she? Is the imp altogether evil? Hath she affections? Hath she any principle of being that can be discovered?"

"None,—save the freedom of a broken law," answered Dimmesdale, quietly, as if he had been discussing the point within himself. "Whether capable of good, I know not."

The child probably overheard their voices; for, looking up to the window, with a bright but naughty smile, she threw one of the prickly burrs at the Reverend Mr. Dimmesdale. The sensitive clergyman shrank, with nervous dread, from the light object. Detecting his emotion, Pearl clapped her little hands in glee. Hester Prynne, likewise, had involuntarily looked up; and all these four persons, old and young, regarded one another in silence, till the child laughed aloud; and shouted,—"Come away, mother! Come away, or yonder old Black Man will catch you! He hath got hold of the minister already. Come away, mother, or he will catch you! But he cannot catch little Pearl!"

So she drew her mother away, skipping, dancing, and frisking fantastically, among the mounds of the dead people, like a creature that had nothing in common with a bygone and buried generation, nor owned herself akin to it.

"There goes a woman," resumed Roger Chillingworth, after a pause, "who, be her faults what they may, hath none of that mystery of hiding sinfulness which you deem so grievous to be borne. Is Hester Prynne less miserable, think you, because of that scarlet letter on her breast?"

"I do verily believe it," answered the clergyman. "Nevertheless I cannot speak for her. There was a look of pain in her face, which I would gladly have been spared the sight of. But, still, methinks, it must needs be better for the sufferer to be free to show his pain, as this poor woman Hester is, than to cover it all up in his heart."

There was another pause; and the physician began anew to examine the plants which he had gathered.

"You inquired of me, a little time ago," said he, at length, "my judgment touching your health."

"I did," answered the clergyman, "and would gladly learn it. Speak frankly, I pray you, be it for life or death."

"Freely, then, and plainly," said the physician, still busy with his plants, but keeping a wary eye on Dimmesdale, "the disorder is a strange one; not so much in itself, nor as outwardly manifested,—in so far, at least, as the symptoms have been laid open to my observation. Looking daily at you, my good Sir, and watching the tokens of your aspect, now for months gone by, I should deem you a very sick man, yet not so sick but that an instructed and watchful physician might well hope to cure you. But—I know not what to say—the disease is what I seem to know, yet know it not."

"You speak in riddles, learned Sir," said the pale minister, glancing aside out of the window.

"Then to speak more plainly," continued the physician, "and I crave pardon, Sir,—should it seem to require pardon,—for this necessary plainness of my speech. Let me ask,—as your friend,—as one having charge, under Providence, of your life and your physical well-being,—hath all the operation of this disorder been fairly laid open and told to me?"

"How can you question it?" asked the minister. "Surely, it were childish to call in a physician, and then hide the sore!"

"You would tell me, then that I know all?" said Roger Chillingworth, deliberately, and fixing an eye, bright with intense and concentrated intelligence, on the minister's face. "Be it so! But, again! He to whom only the outward and physical evil is laid open, knows, oftentimes, but half the evil which he is called upon to cure. A bodily disease, which we look upon as whole and entire within itself, may, after all, be but a symptom of some ailment in the spiritual part. Your pardon, once again, good Sir, if my speech give the shadow of offence. You, Sir, of all men whom I have known, are he whose body is the closest joined, and imbued, and identified, so to speak, with the spirit whereof it is the instrument."

"Then I need ask no further," said the clergyman, somewhat hastily rising from his chair. "You deal not, I take it, in medicine for the soul!"

"Thus, a sickness," continued Roger Chillingworth, without noticing the interruption,—but standing up, and looking at the emaciated and white-cheeked minister, with his low, dark, misshapen figure,—"a sickness, a sore place, if we may so call it, in your spirit, hath immediately its appropriate manifestation⁴ in your bodily frame. Would you, therefore, that your physician heal the bodily evil? How may this be, unless you first lay open to him the wound or trouble in your soul?"

"No!—not to thee!—not to an *earthly* physician!" cried Dimmesdale, passionately, turning his eyes, full and bright, and with a kind of fierceness, on old Roger Chillingworth. "Not to *thee!* But, if it be the soul's disease, then

⁴ manifestation: outward sign

do I commit myself to the one Physician of the soul! He, if it stand with his good pleasure, can cure; or he can kill! Let him do with me, as, in his justice and wisdom, he shall see good. But who art *thou*, that meddlest in this matter?—that dares thrust himself between the sufferer and his God?"

With a frantic gesture he rushed out of the room.

"It is as well to have made this step," said Roger Chillingworth to himself, looking after the minister with a grave smile. "There is nothing lost. We shall be friends again. But see, now, how passion takes hold upon this man, and hurries him out of himself! As with one passion, so with another! He hath done a wild thing erenow, this pious Master Dimmesdale, in the hot passion of his heart!"

It was not difficult to reestablish the intimacy of the two companions, on the same footing and in the same degree as before. The young clergyman, after a few hours of privacy, realized that the disorder of his nerves had made him lose his temper. He marvelled, indeed, at the violence with which he had thrust back the kind old man, who was merely proffering advice which it was his duty to bestow, and which the minister himself had expressly sought. With these remorseful feelings, he lost no time in making the fullest apologies, and begged his friend to continue the care, which, if not successful in restoring him to health, had, at least, been the means of prolonging his feeble existence to that hour. Roger Chillingworth readily assented, and went on with his medical care of the minister; doing his best for him, in all good faith, but always leaving his apartment, at the close of a professional interview, with a mysterious and puzzled smile upon his lips. This expression was invisible in Dimmesdale's presence, but grew strongly evident as the physician crossed the threshold.

"A rare case!" he muttered. "I must needs look deeper into it. A strange sympathy between soul and body! Were it only for the art's sake, I must search this matter to the bottom!"

It came to pass, not long after the scene above recorded, that Dimmesdale, at noonday, and entirely unawares, fell into a deep slumber, sitting in his chair, with a large black-letter[5] volume open before him on the table. The profound depth of the minister's repose was the more remarkable, inasmuch as he was an exceedingly light sleeper. To such an unwonted remoteness, however, had his spirit now withdrawn into itself, that he stirred not in his chair when old Roger Chillingworth, without special precaution, came into the room. The physician approached his patient, laid his hand upon his bosom, and thrust aside the garment that, hitherto, had always covered it, even from the professional eye.

Then, indeed, Dimmesdale shuddered, and stirred slightly.

After a brief pause, the physician removed his hand and turned away.

But with what a wild look of wonder, joy, and horror! With what a ghastly rapture, as it were, too mighty to be expressed only by the eye and features, and therefore bursting forth through the whole ugliness of his figure, and making itself even riotously manifest by the extravagant gestures with which he threw up his arms towards the ceiling, and stamped his foot upon the floor! Had a man seen old Roger Chillingworth, at this moment of his ecstasy, he would have had no need to ask how Satan acts when a precious human soul is lost to heaven, and won into his kingdom.

But what distinguished the physician's ecstasy from Satan's was the trait of wonder in it!

---

[5] black-letter: printed in a heavy type, sometimes called "Old English," that was formerly used for Bibles and other religious books

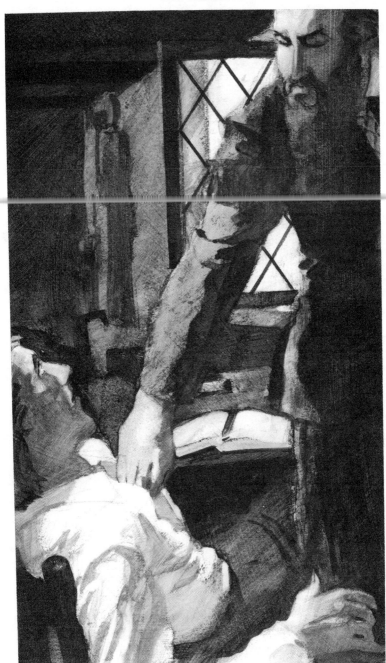

11 *The Interior of a Heart*

After the incident last described, the relationship between the clergyman and the physician, though externally the same, was really of another character than it had previously been. The intellect of Roger Chillingworth had now a plain path before it. It was not, indeed, exactly that which he had laid out for himself to tread. Calm, gentle, without passion, as he appeared, there was yet, we fear, a quiet depth of malice, hitherto latent, but active now, in this unfortunate old man, which led him to imagine a more intimate revenge than any mortal had ever wreaked upon an enemy. To make himself the one trusted friend, to whom should be confided all the fear, the remorse, the agony, the ineffectual repentance, the backward rush of sinful thoughts,—all expelled in vain! All that guilty sorrow, hidden from the world, whose great heart would have pitied and forgiven, to be revealed to him, the Pitiless, to him, the Unforgiving! All that dark treasure to be lavished on the very man, to whom nothing else could so fully pay the debt of vengeance!

The clergyman's shy and sensitive reserve had defeated this scheme. Roger Chillingworth, however, was inclined to be hardly, if at all, less satisfied with the aspect of affairs, which Providence—using the avenger and his victim for its own purposes,—had substituted for his black plans. A revelation, he could almost say, had been granted to him. It mattered little, for his object, whether heavenly, or from what other region. By its aid, in all the subsequent relations between him and Dimmesdale, not merely the external presence, but the very soul, of the latter, seemed to be brought out before his eyes, so that he could see and comprehend its every movement. He became, thenceforth not only a spectator, but a chief actor, in the poor minister's interior world. He could play upon him as he chose. Would he arouse him with a throb of agony? The victim was forever on the rack; it needed only to know the spring that controlled the engine; and that the physician knew well! Would he startle him with sudden fear? As at the waving of a magician's wand, uprose a horrible phantom,—a thousand phantoms,—in many shapes, of death, or more awful shame, all flocking round about the clergyman, and pointing their fingers at his breast!

All this was accomplished with a subtlety so perfect that the minister, though he had constantly a dim feeling of some evil influence watching over him, could never gain a knowledge of its actual nature. True, he looked doubtfully, fearfully,—even, at times, with horror and bitterness of hatred,—at the deformed figure of the old physician. His gestures, his gait, his grizzled beard, his slightest acts, even the very fashion of his garments, were hateful to him; a token implicitly to be relied on, of a deeper hatred in the breast of the latter than he was willing to admit to himself. For, as it was impossible to assign a reason for such distrust and abhorrence, so Dimmesdale, conscious that the poison of one morbid spot was infecting his heart's entire substance, attributed all his presentiments to no other cause. He took himself to task for his feelings in reference to Roger Chillingworth, disregarded the lesson that he should have drawn from them, and did his best to root them out. Unable to accomplish this, he nevertheless, as a matter of principle, continued his habits of social familiarity with the old man, and thus gave him constant opportunities for perfecting the purpose to which—poor, forlorn creature that he was, even more wretched than his victim—the avenger had devoted himself.

While thus suffering under bodily disease, and gnawed and tortured by some black trouble of the soul, and given over to the schemes of his deadliest enemy, the minister had won a brilliant popularity in his sacred office. He won it, indeed, in great part, by his sorrows. His intellectual gifts, his moral perceptions, his power of experiencing and communicating emotion, all were kept in a state of uncommon activity by the anguish of his daily life. His fame, though still on its upward climb, already overshadowed the soberer reputations of his fellow-clergymen, eminent as several of them were. There were scholars among them, who had spent more years in acquiring abstruse lore, connected with the divine profession, than Dimmesdale had lived; and who might well, therefore, be more profoundly versed in such solid and valuable attainments than their youthful brother. There were men, too, of a sturdier texture of mind than his, and endowed with a far greater share of shrewd, hard, iron, or granite understanding. There were others, again, true saintly fathers, whose faculties had been elaborated by weary toil among their books, and by patient thought, and made heavenly, moreover, by spiritual communications with the better world, into which their purity of life had almost introduced these holy personages, with their garments of mortality still clinging to them.

Not improbably, it was to this latter class of men that Dimmesdale, by many of his traits of character, naturally belonged. To the high mountain-peaks of faith and purity he would have climbed, had not the tendency been thwarted by the burden of crime or anguish, beneath which it was his doom to totter. It kept him down, on a level with the lowest; him, the man of holy attributes, whose voice the angels might else have listened to and answered! But this very burden it was that gave him sympathies so intimate with the sinful brotherhood of mankind, so that his heart vibrated in unison with theirs, and received their pain into itself, and sent its own throb of pain through a thousand other hearts, in gushes of sad, persuasive eloquence. Oftenest persuasive, but sometimes terrible! The people knew not the power that moved them thus. They deemed the young clergyman a miracle of holiness. They fancied him the mouthpiece of Heaven's messages of wisdom, and rebuke, and love. In their eyes, the very ground on which he trod was holy. The virgins of his church grew pale around him, victims of a passion so imbued with[1] religious sentiment that they imagined it to be all religion, and brought it openly, in their white bosoms, as their most acceptable sacrifice before the altar. The aged members of his flock, beholding his feeble frame while they were themselves so rugged in their infirmity, believed that he would go to heaven before them, and enjoined it upon their children, that their old bones should be buried close to their young pastor's holy grave.

It is inconceivable, the agony with which this public veneration tortured him! It was his genuine impulse to adore the truth, and to reckon all things shadowlike, and utterly devoid of weight or value, that had not its divine essence as the life within their life. Then, what was he?— a substance?—or the dimmest of all shadows? He longed to speak out, from his own pulpit, at the full height of his voice, and tell the people what he was. "I, whom you behold in these black garments of the priesthood,—I, who ascend the sacred desk, and turn my pale face heavenward, taking upon myself to hold communion, in your behalf,

[1] imbued with: colored by; filled with

with the Most High Omniscience,—I, whose footsteps, as you suppose, leave a gleam along my earthly track, whereby the pilgrims that shall come after me may be guided to the regions of the blest,—I, who have laid the hand of baptism upon your children,—I, who have breathed the parting prayer over your dying friends, to whom the Amen sounded faintly from a world which they have quitted,—I, your pastor, whom you so revere and trust, am utterly a corruption and a lie!"

More than once, Dimmesdale had gone into the pulpit with a purpose never to come down its steps until he had spoken words like the above. More than once, he had cleared his throat, and drawn in the long, deep, and tremulous breath, which, when sent forth again, would come burdened with the black secret of his soul. More than once—nay, more than a hundred times—he had actually spoken! Spoken? But how? He had told his hearers that he was altogether vile, a viler companion of the vilest, the worst of sinners, an abomination, a thing of unimaginable iniquity; and that the only wonder was that they did not see his wretched body shrivelled up before their eyes, by the burning wrath of the Almighty! Could there be plainer speech than this? Would not the people start up in their seats, by a simultaneous impulse, and tear him down out of the pulpit, which he defiled? Not so, indeed! They heard it all, and did but reverence him the more. They little guessed what deadly purport lurked in those self-condemning words. "The godly youth!" said they among themselves. "The saint on earth! Alas, if he see such sinfulness in his own white soul, what horrid spectacle would he behold in thine or mine!" The minister well knew—subtle, but remorseful hypocrite that he was!—the light in which vague confession would be viewed. He had spoken the very truth, and transformed it into the veriest falsehood. And yet, he loved the truth, and loathed the lie, as few men ever did. Therefore, above all things else, he loathed his miserable self!

His inward trouble drove him to practices more in accordance with the old, corrupted faith of Rome, than with the better light of the church in which he had been born and bred. In his secret closet, under lock and key, there was a bloody whip. Oftentimes, this Protestant and Puritan divine had plied it on his own shoulders; laughing bitterly at himself the while, and smiting so much the more pitilessly because of that bitter laugh. It was his custom, too, as it has been that of many other pious Puritans, to fast,—not in order to purify the body and render it the fitter medium of celestial illumination, but rigorously, and until his knees trembled beneath him, as an act of penance. He kept vigils, likewise, night after night, sometimes in utter darkness; sometimes with a glimmering lamp; and sometimes, viewing his own face in a looking-glass, by the most powerful light which he could throw upon it. He thus typified the constant introspection wherewith he tortured, but could not purify, himself. In these lengthened vigils, his brain often reeled, and visions seemed to flit before him; perhaps seen doubtfully, and by a faint light of their own, in the remote dimness of the chamber, or more vividly, and close beside him, with the glass. Now it was a herd of devilish shapes, that grinned and mocked at the pale minister, and beckoned him away with them; now a group of shining angels, who flew upward heavily, as sorrow-laden, but grew more ethereal as they rose. Now came the dead friends of his youth, and his white-bearded father, with a saint-like frown, and his mother, turning her face away, as she passed by. Ghost of a mother,—methinks she might have yet thrown a pitying glance towards her son! And now, through the chamber which these spectral thoughts had made so ghastly, glided Hester Prynne, leading little Pearl, in her scarlet garb, and pointing her finger, first at the scarlet letter on her bosom, and then at the clergyman's own breast.

None of these visions ever quite deluded him. At any moment, by an effort of his will, he could discern substances through their misty lack of substance, and convince himself that they were not solid in their nature, like that table of carved oak, or that big, square, leathern-bound and bronze volume of divinity. But, for all that, they were, in one sense, the truest and most substantial things which the poor minister now dealt with. It is the unspeakable misery of a life so false as his, that it steals the heart out of whatever realities there are around us. To the untrue man, the whole universe is false,—it shrinks to nothing within his grasp. And he himself, in so far as he shows himself in a false light, becomes a shadow, or ceases to exist. The only truth that continued to give Dimmesdale a real existence on earth was the anguish in his soul, and the open expression of it in his aspect. Had he once found power to smile, and wear a face of gayety, there would have been no such man!

On one of those ugly nights, which we have faintly hinted at, but hesitated to describe, the minister started from his chair. A new thought had struck him! There might be a moment's peace in it. Attiring himself with as much care as if for public worship, and precisely in the same manner, he stole softly down the staircase, undid the door, and went out.

12 *The Minister's Vigil*

Walking in the shadow of a dream, as it were, and perhaps actually under the influence of a type of sleep-walking, Dimmesdale reached the spot where, now so long since, Hester Prynne had lived through her first hours of public shame. The same platform, black and weather-stained with the storm or sunshine of seven long years, and foot-worn, too, with the tread of many culprits who had since ascended it, remained standing beneath the balcony of the meeting house. The minister went up the steps.

It was an obscure night in early May. An unvaried pall of cloud muffled the whole expanse of sky from zenith to horizon. If the same multitude which had stood as eye-witnesses while Hester Prynne sustained her punishment could now have been summoned forth, they would have seen no face above the platform, nor hardly the outline of a human shape, in the dark gray of the midnight. But the town was asleep. There was no danger of discovery. The minister might stand there, if it pleased him, until morning, without other risk than that the dank and chill night air would creep into his frame, stiffen his joints with rheumatism, and clog his throat with catarrh and cough; thereby defrauding the expectant audience of to-morrow's prayer and sermon. No eye could see him, save that ever-wakeful one which had seen him in his closet, wielding the bloody whip. Why, then, had he come hither? Was it but a mockery of penitence? A mockery, indeed, but in which his soul trifled with itself! A mockery at which angels blushed and wept, while fiends rejoiced, with jeering laughter! He had been driven hither by the impulse of that Remorse which followed him everywhere, and whose own sister and closely linked companion was that Cowardice which always drew him back, with her tremulous grip, just when the other impulse had hurried him to the verge of disclosure. Poor, miserable man! what right had infirmity like his to burden itself with crime? Crime is for the iron-nerved, who have their choice either to endure it, or, if it press too hard, to exert their fierce and savage strength for a good purpose, and fling it off at once!

And thus, while standing on the scaffold, in this vain show of expiation, Dimmesdale was overcome with horror, as if the universe were gazing at a scarlet token on his naked breast, right over his heart. On that spot, in very truth, there was, and there had long been, the gnawing and poisonous tooth of bodily pain. Without any effort of his will, or power to restrain himself, he shrieked aloud; an outcry that went pealing through the night, and was beaten back from one house to another, and echoed from the hills in the background; as if a company of devils, detecting so much misery and terror in it, had made a plaything of the sound, and were bandying[1] it to and fro.

"It is done!" muttered the minister, covering his face. "The whole town will awake, and hurry forth, and find me here! It is done!"

But it was not so. The shriek had perhaps sounded with a far greater power, to his own startled ears, than it actually possessed. The town did *not* awake; or, if it did, the drowsy sleepers mistook the cry either for something frightful in a dream, or for the noise of witches; whose

[1] bandying: tossing

voices, at that period, were often heard to pass over the settlements or lonely cottages, as they rode with Satan through the air. The clergyman, therefore, hearing no signs of disturbance, uncovered his eyes and looked about him. At one of the chamber-windows of Governor Belling-ham's mansion, which stood at some distance, on the line of another street, he beheld the old magistrate himself, with a lamp in his hand, a white nightcap on his head, and a long white gown enveloping his figure. He looked like a ghost, called unseasonably from the grave. The cry had evidently startled him. At another window of the same house, moreover, appeared old Mistress Hibbins, the Governor's sister, also with a lamp, which, even thus far off, revealed the expression of her sour face. She thrust forth her head from the lattice, and looked anxiously upward. Beyond the shadow of a doubt, this venerable witch-lady had heard Dimmesdale's outcry, and interpreted it, with its countless echoes and reverberations, as the clamor of the fiends and night-hags, with whom she was well known to make excursions into the forest.

Detecting the gleam of Governor Bellingham's lamp, the old lady quickly extinguished her own, and vanished. Possibly, she went up among the clouds. The minister saw nothing further of her motions. The magistrate, after a careful observation of the outer darkness, retired from the window.

The minister grew comparatively calm. His eyes, how-ever, were soon greeted by a little, glimmering light, which, at first a long way off, was approaching up the street. It threw a gleam of recognition on here a post, and there a garden-fence, here a latticed window-pane, and there a pump, with its full trough of water, and here, again, an arched door of oak, with an iron knocker, and a rough log for the doorstep. Dimmesdale noted all these minute par-ticulars, even while firmly convinced that the doom of his existence was stealing onward, in the footstep which he now heard; and that the gleam of the lantern would fall upon him, in a few moments, and reveal his long-hidden secret. As the light drew nearer, he beheld, within its illuminated circle, his brother clergyman,—or to speak more accurately, his professional father, as well as highly valued friend,—the Reverend Mr. Wilson; who, as Dimmesdale now conjectured, had been praying at the bedside of some dying man. And so he had. The good old minister came freshly from the death-chamber of Governor Winthrop,[2] who had passed from earth to heaven within that very hour. And now, surrounded, like the saint-like personages of olden times, with a radiant halo, that glorified him amid this gloomy night of sin, now good Father Wilson was moving homeward, aiding his footsteps with a lighted lantern! The glimmer of this luminary suggested the above thoughts to Dimmesdale, who smiled,—nay, almost laughed at them,—and then wondered if he were going mad.

As the Reverend Mr. Wilson passed beside the scaffold, closely muffling his cloak about him with one arm, and holding the lantern before his breast with the other, the minister could hardly restrain himself from speaking.

"A good evening to you, venerable Father Wilson! Come up hither, I pray you, and pass here a pleasant hour with me!"

Good heavens! Had Dimmesdale actually spoken? For one instant, he believed that these words had passed his lips. But they were spoken only with his imagination. The venerable Father Wilson continued to step slowly onward, looking carefully at the muddy pathway before his feet, and never once turning his head towards the guilty platform. When the light of the glimmering lantern had faded quite away, the minister discovered, by the faintness which

---

[2] Winthrop: John Winthrop, first governor of the Massachusetts Colony

came over him, that the last few moments had been a crisis of terrible anxiety; although his mind had made an involuntary effort to relieve itself by a kind of lurid[3] playfulness.

Shortly afterwards, the like grisly sense of the humorous again stole in among the solemn phantoms of his thought. He felt his limbs growing stiff with the unaccustomed chilliness of the night, and doubted whether he should be able to descend the steps of the scaffold. Morning would break, and he would be found there. The neighborhood would begin to rouse itself. The earliest riser, coming forth in the dim twilight, would perceive a vaguely defined figure aloft on the place of shame; and, half-crazed betwixt alarm and curiosity, would go, knocking from door to door, summoning all the people to behold the ghost—as he needs must think of it—of some dead sinner. Then—the morning light still waxing stronger—old patriarchs would rise up in great haste, each in his flannel gown, and matronly dames, without pausing to put off their night-gear. The whole tribe of decorous personages, who had never heretofore been seen with a single hair of their heads awry, would start into public view, with all the disorder of a nightmare in their aspects. Old Governor Bellingham would come grimly forth, with his King James's ruff fastened askew; and Mistress Hibbins, with some twigs of the forest clinging to her skirts, and looking more sour than ever, as having hardly got a wink of sleep after her night ride; and good Father Wilson, too, after spending half the night, at a deathbed, and liking ill to be disturbed, thus early, out of his dreams about the glorified saints. Hither, likewise, would come the elders and deacons of Dimmesdale's church, and the young virgins who so idolized their minister, and had made a shrine for him in their white bosoms. All people, in a word, would come stumbling

---

[3] lurid: wan, feeble

over their thresholds, and turning up their amazed and horror-stricken visages around the scaffold. Whom would they discern there, with the red eastern light upon his brow? Whom, but the Reverend Arthur Dimmesdale, half frozen to death, overwhelmed with shame, and standing where Hester Prynne had stood!

Carried away by the grotesque horror of this picture, the minister burst into wild laughter. It was immediately responded to by a light, airy, childish laugh, in which, with a thrill of the heart,—but he knew not whether of exquisite pain, or pleasure as acute,—he recognized the tones of Little Pearl.

"Pearl! Little Pearl!" cried he after a moment's cause; then, suppressing his voice,—"Hester! Hester Prynne! Are you there?"

"Yes; it is Hester Prynne!" she replied, in a tone of surprise; and the minister heard her footsteps approaching from the sidewalk, along which she had been passing. "It is I, and my little Pearl."

"Whence come you, Hester?" asked the minister.

"I have been watching at a death-bed," answered Hester Prynne,—"at Governor Winthrop's death-bed, and have taken his measure for a robe, and am now going home."

"Come up hither, Hester, thou and little Pearl. Ye have both been here before, but I was not with you. Come up hither once again, and we will stand all three together!"

She silently ascended the steps, and stood on the platform, holding Pearl by the hand. The minister felt for the child's other hand, and took it. The moment that he did so, there came what seemed a tumultuous rush of new life, other life than his own, pouring like a torrent into his heart, and hurrying through all his veins, as if the mother and the child were communicating their vital warmth to his half-torpid system. The three formed an electric chain. "Minister!" whispered little Pearl.

"What wouldst thou say, child?" asked Dimmesdale.

"Wilt thou stand here with mother and me, to-morrow at noon?" inquired Pearl.

"Nay, not so, my little Pearl," answered the minister; for with the new energy of the moment, all the dread of public exposure, that had so long been the anguish of his life, returned upon him; and he was already trembling at the position in which—with a strange joy, nevertheless—he now found himself. "Not so, my child. I shall, indeed, stand with thy mother and thee, one other day, but not to-morrow."

Pearl laughed, and attempted to pull away her hand. But the minister held it fast.

"A moment longer, my child!" said he.

"But wilt thou promise," asked Pearl, "to take my hand and mother's hand to-morrow noontide?"

"Not then, Pearl," said the minister, "but another time."

"And what other time?" persisted the child.

"At the great Judgment Day," whispered the minister,—and strangely enough, the sense that he was a professional teacher of the truth impelled him to answer the child so. "Then, and there, before the judgment-seat, thy mother, and thou, and I must stand together. But the daylight of this world shall not see our meeting!"

Pearl laughed again.

But before he finished speaking, a light gleamed far and wide over all the muffled sky. It was doubtless caused by one of those meteors, which the night-watcher may so often observe, burning out to waste, in the vacant regions of the atmosphere. So powerful was its radiance, that it thoroughly illuminated the dense medium of cloud between the sky and earth. The great vault brightened, like the dome of an immense lamp. It showed the familiar scene of the street, with the distinctness of midday, but also with the awfulness that is always imparted to familiar objects by an unaccustomed light. The wooden houses, with their jutting stories and quaint gable-peaks; the door-steps and thresholds, with the early grass springing up about them; the garden-plots, black with freshly-turned earth; the wheel-track, little worn, and, even in the market place, margined with green on either side,—all were visible, but with a strangeness of aspect that seemed to give another moral interpretation to the things of this world than they had ever had before. And there stood the minister, with his hand over his heart; Hester Prynne, with the embroidered letter glimmering on her bosom; and little Pearl, herself a symbol, and the connecting link between those two. They stood in the noon of that strange and solemn splendor, as if it were the light that is to reveal all secrets, and the daybreak that shall unite all who belong to one another.

There was witchcraft in little Pearl's eyes, and her face, as she glanced upward at the minister, wore that naughty smile which made its expression elfish. She withdrew her hand from Dimmesdale's, and pointed across the street. But he clasped both his hands over his breast, and cast his eyes towards the zenith.

Nothing was more common, in those days, than to interpret all meteoric appearances, and other natural phenomena, as so many revelations from a supernatural source. Thus, a blazing spear, a sword of flame, a bow, or a sheaf of arrows, seen in the midnight sky, foretold Indian warfare. Pestilence was known to have been foretold by a shower of crimson light. We doubt whether any marked event, for good or evil, ever befell New England, from its settlement on down to Revolutionary times, of which the inhabitants had not been previously warned by a spectacle of this nature. Not seldom, it had been seen by multitudes. Oftener, however, its belief rested on the faith of a lonely eye-witness, who beheld the wonder through the colored, magnifying, and distorting medium of his imagination, and shaped it more distinctly in his after-thought. It was, indeed, a majestic idea, that the destiny of nations should be revealed, in these awful signs, on the cope of heaven. The belief was a favorite one with our forefathers, as indicating that their infant commonwealth was under a celestial guardianship of peculiar intimacy and strictness. But what shall we say, when an individual discovers a revelation addressed to himself alone! In such a case, it could only be the symptom of a highly disordered mental state, when a man, made morbidly self-contemplative by long, intense, and secret pain, had extended his egotism over the whole expanse of nature, until the firmament itself should appear no more than a fitting page for his soul's history and fate!

We impute it, therefore, solely to the disease in his own eye and heart, that the minister, looking upward to the zenith, beheld there an immense letter,—the letter A,— marked out in lines of dull red light. Not but the meteor may have shown itself at that point, burning duskily through a veil of cloud; but with no such shape as his guilty imagination gave it; or, at least, with so little definiteness, that another's guilt might have seen another symbol in it.

There was a strange circumstance that characterized Dimmesdale's psychological state at this moment. All the time that he gazed upward, he was, nevertheless, perfectly aware that little Pearl was pointing her finger towards old Roger Chillingworth, who stood at no great distance from the scaffold. The minister appeared to see him, with the same glance that discerned the miraculous letter. To his features, as to all other objects, the meteoric light imparted a new expression; or it might be that the physician was not careful then, as at all other times, to hide the ill-will with which he looked upon his victim. Certainly, if the meteor kindled up the sky, and disclosed the earth, with an awfulness that warned Hester and the clergyman of the day of judgment, then might Roger Chillingworth have passed with them for the arch-fiend, standing there with a smile and scowl to claim his own. So vivid was the expression, or so intense the minister's perception of it, that it seemed still to remain painted on the darkness, after the meteor had vanished, with an effect as if the street and all things else were at once annihilated.

"Who is that man, Hester?" gasped Dimmesdale, overcome with terror. "I shiver at him! Dost thou know the man? I hate him, Hester!"

She remembered her oath, and was silent.

"I tell thee, my soul shivers at him!" muttered the minister again. "Who is he? Who is he? Canst thou do nothing for me? I have a nameless horror of the man!"

"Minister," said little Pearl, "I can tell thee who he is!"

"Quickly, then, child!" said the minister, bending his ear close to her lips. "Quickly!—and as low as thou canst whisper."

Pearl mumbled something into his ear, that sounded, indeed, like human language, but was only such gibberish as children amuse themselves with, by the hour together. At all events, if it involved any secret information in regard to old Roger Chillingworth, it was in a tongue unknown to the learned clergyman, and did but increase his bewilderment. The elfish child then laughed aloud.

"Dost thou mock me now?" asked the minister.

"You were not bold!—you were not true!"—answered the child. "You would not promise to take my hand, and my mother's hand, to-morrow noontide!"

"Worthy Sir," answered the physician, who had now advanced to the foot of the platform. "Pious Master Dimmesdale, can this be you? Well, well, indeed! We men of study, whose heads are in our books, need to be looked after! We dream in our waking moments, and walk in our sleep. Come, good Sir, and my dear friend, I pray you, let me lead you home!"

"How knewest thou that I was here?" asked the minister, fearfully.

"Verily, and in good faith," answered Roger Chillingworth, "I knew nothing of the matter. I was at the bedside of Governor Winthrop, doing what my poor skill might to give him ease. I was on my way homeward, when this strange light shone out. Come with me, I beseech you, Reverend Sir; else you will be poorly able to do Sabbath duty to-morrow."

"I will go home with you," said Dimmesdale.

With a chill despondency, like one awakening, all nerveless, from an ugly dream, he yielded himself to the physician and was led away.

The next day, however, being the Sabbath, he preached a discourse which was held to be the richest and most powerful, and the most replete with heavenly influences, that had ever proceeded from his lips. But, as he came down the pulpit steps, the gray-bearded sexton[4] met him, holding up a black glove, which the minister recognized as his own.

"It was found," said the sexton, "this morning, on the scaffold where evil-doers are set up to public shame. Satan dropped it there, I take it, intending a scurrilous jest against your reverence. But, indeed, he was blind and foolish, as he ever and always is. A pure hand needs no glove to cover it!"

"Thank you, my good friend," said the minister, gravely, but startled at heart; for so confused was his remembrance, that he had almost brought himself to look at

[4] sexton: a church official in charge of the maintenance of church property

the events of the past night as visionary. "Yes, it seems to be my glove, indeed!"

"And, since Satan saw fit to steal it, your reverence must needs handle him without gloves, henceforward," remarked the old sexton, grimly smiling. "But did your reverence hear of the portent that was seen last night? a great red letter in the sky,—the letter A, which we interpret to stand for Angel. For, as our good Governor Winthrop was made an angel this past night, it was doubtless held fit that there should be some notice thereof!"

"No," answered the minister, "I did not hear of it."

13 *Another View of Hester*

In her late singular interview[1] with Dimmesdale, Hester Prynne was shocked at the condition in which she found the clergyman. His nerve seemed absolutely destroyed. His moral force was abased into more than childish weakness. It grovelled helpless on the ground, even while his intellectual faculties retained their original strength, or had perhaps acquired a morbid energy, which disease only could have given them. With her knowledge of a train of circumstances hidden from all others, she could readily infer that, besides the legitimate action of his own conscience, a terrible machinery had been brought to bear, and was still operating, on his well-being and repose. Knowing what this poor, fallen man had once been, her whole soul was moved by the shuddering terror with which he had appealed to her,—the outcast woman,—for support against his instinctively discovered enemy. She decided, moreover, that he had a right to her utmost aid. Little accustomed, in her long seclusion from society, to measure her ideas of right and wrong by any standard outside of herself, Hester saw that there lay a responsibility upon her, in regard to the clergyman, which she owed to no other, nor to the whole world besides. The links that united her to the rest of humanity—links of flowers, or silk, or gold,

[1] interview: face-to-face meeting

or whatever the material—had all been broken. Here was the iron link of mutual crime, which neither he nor she could break. Like all other ties, it brought along with it its obligations.

Hester Prynne did not now occupy precisely the same position in which we beheld her during the earlier periods of her disgrace. Years had come and gone. Pearl was now seven. Her mother, with the scarlet letter on her breast, glittering in its fantastic embroidery, had long been a familiar object to the townspeople. As is apt to be the case when a person stands out in any prominence before the community, and, at the same time, interferes neither with public nor individual interests and convenience, a species of general regard had ultimately grown up in reference to Hester Prynne. It is to the credit of human nature, that, except where its selfishness is brought into play, it loves more readily than it hates. Hatred, by a gradual and quiet process, will even be transformed to love, unless the change be impeded by a new irritation of the original feeling of hostility. In this matter of Hester Prynne, there was no irritation. She never battled with the public, but submitted, uncomplainingly, to its worst usage; she made no claim upon it, in return for what she suffered; she did not weigh upon its sympathies. Then, also, the blameless purity of her life during all these years in which she had been set apart to infamy, was reckoned in her favor. With nothing now to lose, and with no hope, and seemingly no wish, of gaining anything, it could only be a genuine regard for virtue that had brought back the poor wanderer to its paths.

It was perceived, too, that while Hester never put forward even the humblest claim to share in the world's privileges,—further than to breathe the common air, and earn daily bread for little Pearl and herself by the faithful labor of her hands,—she was quick to acknowledge her sisterhood with the race of man, whenever benefits were to be conferred. None so ready as she to give of her little substance to every demand of poverty; even though the bitter-hearted pauper threw back a gibe in return for the food brought regularly to his door, or the garments wrought for him by the fingers that could have embroidered a monarch's robe. None so self-devoted as Hester, when disease stalked through the town. In all seasons of calamity, indeed, whether general or of individuals, the outcast of society at once found her place. She came, not as a guest, but as a rightful inmate, into the household darkened by trouble; as if its gloomy twilight were a medium in which she was entitled to converse with her fellow-creatures. There glimmered the embroidered letter, with comfort in its unearthly ray. Elsewhere the token of sin, it was the candle of the sick-chamber. It had even thrown its gleam, in the sufferer's hard extremity, across the verge of time. It had shown him where to set his foot, while the light of earth was fast becoming dim, and before the light of futurity could reach him. In such emergencies, Hester's nature showed itself warm and rich. Her breast, with its badge of shame, was but the softer pillow for the head that needed one. She was self-ordained a Sister of Mercy; or, we may rather say, the world's heavy hand had so ordained her, when neither the world nor she looked forward to this result. The letter was the symbol of her calling. Such helpfulness was found in her,—so much power to do, and power to sympathize,—that many people refused to interpret the scarlet A by its original signification. They said it meant Able; so strong was Hester Prynne, with a woman's strength.

It was only the darkened house that could contain her. When sunshine came again, she was not there. Her shadow had faded across the threshold. The helpful inmate had departed, without one backward glance to gather up the reward of gratitude, if any were in the hearts of those whom she had served so zealously. Meeting them in the street, she never raised her head to receive their greeting. If they were determined to greet her, she laid her finger on the scarlet letter and passed on. This might be pride, but was so like humility, that it produced all the softening influence of the latter quality. The public is despotic in its temper; it is capable of denying common justice, when demanded as a right; but quite as frequently it awards *more than* justice, when the appeal is made, as despots love to have it made, to its generosity. Interpreting Hester Prynne's conduct as an appeal of this nature, society was inclined to show its former victim a more friendly countenance than she cared to be favored with, or, perchance, than she deserved.

The rulers, and the wise and learned men of the community, were longer in acknowledging the influence of Hester's good qualities than the people. The prejudices which they shared in common with the latter were fortified in themselves by an iron framework of reasoning, that made it harder to expel them. Day by day, nevertheless, their sour and rigid wrinkles were relaxing into something which, in the due course of years, might grow to be an expression of almost benevolence. Thus it was with the men of rank, on whom their eminent position imposed the guardianship of the public morals. Individuals in private life, meanwhile, had quite forgiven Hester Prynne for her frailty; nay, more, they had begun to look upon the scarlet letter as the token, not of that one sin, for which she had borne so long and dreary a penance, but of her many good deeds since. "Do you see that woman with the embroidered badge?" they would say to strangers. "It is our Hester,— the town's own Hester, who is so kind to the poor, so helpful to the sick, so comfortable to the afflicted!" Then, it is true, the habit of human nature to tell the very worst of itself, when embodied in the person of another, would

urge them to whisper the black scandal of bygone years. It was none the less a fact, however, that, in the eyes of the very men who spoke thus, the scarlet letter had the effect of the cross on a nun's bosom. It imparted to the wearer a kind of sacredness, which enabled her to walk securely amid all peril. Had she fallen among thieves, it would have kept her safe. It was reported, and believed, by many, that an Indian had drawn his arrow against the badge, and that the missile struck it, but fell harmless to the ground.

The effect of the symbol,—or, rather, of the position in respect to society that was indicated by it—on the mind of Hester Prynne herself, was powerful and peculiar. All the light and graceful foliage of her character had been withered up by this red-hot brand, and had long ago fallen away, leaving a bare and harsh outline, which might have been repulsive, had she possessed any friends or companions to be repelled by it. Even the attractiveness of her person had undergone a similar change. It might be partly owing to the studied plainness of her dress, and partly to the lack of demonstration in her manners. It was a sad transformation, too, that her rich, luxuriant hair had either been cut off, or was completely hidden by a cap, so that not a shining lock of it ever once gushed into the sunshine. It was due in part to all these causes, but still more to something else, that there seemed to be no longer anything in Hester's face for Love to dwell upon; nothing in Hester's form, that Passion would ever dream of clasping in its embrace; nothing in Hester's bosom, to make it ever again the pillow of Affection. Some quality had departed from her, the permanence of which had been essential to keep her a woman. Such is frequently the fate, and such the stern development, of the feminine character and person, when the woman has lived through an experience of peculiar severity. If she be all tenderness, she will die. If she live, the tenderness will either be crushed out of her, or crushed so deeply into her heart that it can never show itself again. The latter is perhaps the truest theory. She who has once been woman, and ceased to be so, might at any moment become a woman again if there is only the magic touch to effect the transfiguration. We shall see whether Hester Prynne were ever afterwards so touched, and so transfigured.

It is remarkable that persons who speculate the most boldly often conform most completely to the external regulations of society. The thought suffices them, without investing itself in the flesh and blood of action. So it seemed to be with Hester. Yet, had little Pearl never come to her from the spiritual world, it might have been far otherwise. Then, she might have come down to us in history, hand in hand with Anne Hutchinson, as the foundress of a religious sect. She might have been a prophetess. She might have suffered death from the stern tribunals of the period, for attempting to undermine the foundations of the Puritan establishment. But, in the education of her child, the mother's enthusiasm of thought had something to wreak itself upon. Providence, in the person of this little girl, had assigned to Hester's charge the germ and blossom of womanhood, to be cherished and developed amid a host of difficulties. Everything was against her. The world was against her. The child's own nature had something wrong in it, which continually betokened that she had been born amiss,—the result of her mother's lawless passion,—and often impelled Hester to ask, in bitterness of heart, whether it were for ill or good that the poor little creature had been born at all.

Indeed, the same dark question often rose into her mind, with reference to the whole race of womanhood. Was existence worth accepting, even to the happiest among them? As concerned her own individual existence, she had long ago decided in the negative, and dismissed the question as settled. As concerned her child, at times, a fearful doubt possessed her soul, whether it were not better to send Pearl at once to heaven, and go herself to such futurity as Eternal Justice should provide.

The scarlet letter had not done its office.

Now, however, her interview with Dimmesdale, on the night of his vigil, had given her a new theme of reflection, and held up to her an object that appeared worthy of any exertion and sacrifice for its attainment. She had witnessed the intense misery beneath which the minister struggled, or, to speak more accurately, had ceased to struggle. She saw that he stood on the verge of lunacy, if he had not already stepped across it. It was impossible to doubt, that, whatever painful value there might be in the secret sting of remorse, a deadlier venom had been infused into it by the hand that offered relief. A secret enemy had been continually by his side, under the guise of a friend and helper, and had availed himself of the opportunities thus afforded for tampering with the delicate springs of his nature. Hester could not but ask herself, whether there had not originally been a defect of truth, courage, and loyalty, on her own part, in allowing the minister to be thrown into a position where so much evil was to be feared, and nothing good to be hoped. Her only justification lay in the fact, that she had been able to discern no method of rescuing him from a blacker ruin than had overwhelmed herself, except by agreeing to Roger Chillingworth's scheme of disguise. Under that impulse, she had made her choice, and had chosen, as it now appeared, the more wretched alternative of the two. She determined to redeem her error, so far as she could. Strengthened by years of hard and solemn trial, she felt herself no longer unable to cope with Roger Chillingworth as on *that* night, abased by sin, and half maddened by the shame that was still new, when they had talked together in the prison-chamber. She had climbed her way, since *then,* to a higher point. The old man, on the other hand, had brought himself nearer to her level, or perhaps below it, by the revenge which he had stooped for.

In short, Hester Prynne resolved to meet her former husband, and do what might be in her power to rescue the victim on whom he had so evidently set his clutch. The occasion was not long in coming. One afternoon, walking with Pearl in a retired part of the peninsula, she beheld the old physician, with a basket on one arm, and a staff in the other hand, stooping along the ground, in quest of roots and herbs for his medicines.

14 *Hester and the Physician*

Hester told little Pearl to run down to the margin of the water, and play with the shells and tangled seaweed, until she had talked awhile with yonder gatherer of herbs. So the child flew away like a bird, and, baring her small white feet, went pattering along the moist margin of the sea. Here and there she stopped, and peeped curiously into a pool, left by the retiring tide as a mirror for Pearl to see her face in. Forth peeped at her, out of the pool, with dark, glistening curls around her head, and an elf-smile in her eyes, the image of a little maid, whom Pearl, having no other playmate, invited to take her hand, and run a race with her. But the visionary little maid, on her part, beckoned likewise, as if to say,—"This is a better place! Come *thou* into the pool!" And Pearl, stepping in, beheld her own white feet at the bottom; while, out of a still lower depth, came the gleam of a kind of fragmentary smile, floating to and fro in the water.

Meanwhile her mother had approached the physician.

"I would speak a word with you," said she,—"a word that concerns us much."

"Aha! and is it Mistress Hester that has a word for old Roger Chillingworth?" answered he, raising himself from his stooping posture. "With all my heart! Why, Mistress, I hear good tidings of you on all hands! No longer ago than yester-eve, a magistrate, a very wise and godly man, was discussing your affairs, Mistress Hester, and told me that there had been question concerning you in the council. It was debated whether or no, with safety to the common weal, yonder scarlet letter might be taken off your bosom. On my life, Hester, I made my entreaty to the worshipful magistrate that it might be done forthwith!"

"It lies not in the pleasure of the magistrates to take off this badge," calmly replied Hester. "Were I worthy to be quit of it, it would fall away of its own nature."

"Nay, then, wear it, if it suits you better," rejoined he. "A woman must follow her own fancy, touching the adornment of her body. The letter is gayly embroidered, and shows right bravely[1] on your bosom!"

All this while, Hester had been looking steadily at the old man, and was shocked to discern what a change had been wrought upon him within the past seven years. It was not so much that he had grown older; for though traces of advancing life were visible, he wore his age well, and seemed to retain a wiry vigor and alertness. But the former aspect of a studious man, calm and quiet, which was what she best remembered in him, had altogether vanished, and been succeeded by an eager, searching, almost fierce, yet carefully guarded, look. It seemed to be his wish and purpose to mask this expression with a smile; but the latter played him false, and flickered over his face so derisively, that the spectator could see his blackness all the better for it. Ever and anon, too, there came a glare of red light out of his eyes; as if the old man's soul were on fire, and kept on smouldering duskily within his breast, until, by some casual puff of passion, it was blown into a momentary flame. This he repressed, as speedily as possible, and strove to look as if nothing of the kind had happened.

In a word, old Roger Chillingworth was a striking

---

[1] bravely: colorfully

evidence of man's ability to transform himself into a devil, if he will only, for a reasonable space of time, undertake a devil's task. This unhappy person had effected such a transformation, by devoting himself, for seven years, to the constant analysis of a heart full of torture, and deriving his enjoyment thence, and adding fuel to those fiery tortures which he analyzed and gloated over.

The scarlet letter burned on Hester Prynne's bosom. Here was another ruin, the responsibility of which came partly home to her.

"What see you in my face," asked the physician, "that you look at it so earnestly?"

"Something that would make me weep, if there were any tears bitter enough for it," answered she. "But let it pass! It is of yonder miserable man that I would speak."

"And what of him?" cried Roger Chillingworth, eagerly, as if he loved the topic, and were glad of an opportunity to discuss it with the only person of whom he could make a confidant. "Not to hide the truth, Mistress Hester, my thoughts happen just now to be busy with the gentleman. So speak freely, and I will make answer."

"When we last spoke together," said Hester, "now seven years ago, it was your pleasure to extort a promise of secrecy, concerning the former relationship of man and wife betwixt yourself and me. As the life and good fame of yonder man were in your hands, there seemed no choice to me, save to be silent, in accordance with your command. Yet it was not without heavy doubts that I thus bound myself; for, having cast off all duty towards other human beings, there remained a duty towards him; and something told me that I was betraying it, in pledging myself to keep your counsel. Since that day, no man is so near to him as you. *You* tread behind his every footstep. *You* are beside him, sleeping and waking. *You* search his thoughts. *You* burrow and rankle in his heart! Your clutch is on his life, and you cause him to die daily a living death; and still he knows you not. In permitting this, I have surely acted a false part by the only man to whom the power was left me to be true!"

"What choice had you?" asked Roger Chillingworth. "My finger, pointed at this man, would have hurled him from his pulpit into a dungeon,—thence, perhaps, to the gallows!"

"It had been better so!" said Hester Prynne.

"What evil have I done the man?" asked Roger Chillingworth again. "I tell thee, Hester Prynne, the richest fee that ever physician earned from monarch could not have bought such care as I have wasted on this miserable priest! But for my aid, his life would have burned away in torments, within the first two years after the perpetration of his crime and thine. For, Hester, his spirit lacked the strength that could have borne up, as thine has, beneath a burden like thy scarlet letter. Oh, I could reveal a goodly secret! But enough! What medical skill can do, I have exhausted on him. That he now breathes, and creeps about on earth, is owing all to me!"

"Better he had died at once!" said Hester Prynne.

"Yea, woman, thou sayest truly!" cried old Roger Chillingworth, letting the lurid fire of his heart blaze out before her eyes. "Better had he died at once! Never did mortal suffer what this man has suffered. And all, all, in the sight of his worst enemy! He has been conscious of me. He has felt an influence dwelling always upon him like a curse. He knew, by some spiritual sense,—for the Creator never made another being so sensitive,—he knew that no friendly hand was pulling at his heart-strings, and that an eye was looking curiously into him, which sought only evil, and found it. But he knew not that the eye and hand were *mine!* With the superstition common to his priestly brotherhood, he fancied himself given over to some fiend, to be tortured with frightful dreams, desperate thoughts, the sting of remorse, and despair of pardon; as a foretaste of what awaits him beyond the grave. But it was the constant shadow of my presence!—the closeness of the man whom he had most vilely wronged!—and who had grown to exist only by this perpetual poison of the direst revenge! Yea, indeed!—he did not err!—there was a fiend at his elbow! A mortal man, with once a human heart, has become a fiend for his especial torment!"

The unfortunate physician, while uttering these words, lifted his hands with a look of horror, as if he had beheld some frightful shape, which he could not recognize, usurping the place of his own image in a glass. Not improbably, he had never before viewed himself as he did just now.

"Hast thou not tortured him enough?" said Hester, noticing the old man's look. "Hast he not paid thee all?"

"No!—no! He has but increased the debt!" answered the physician; and as he proceeded, his manner lost its fiercer characteristics, and subsided into gloom. "Dost thou remember me, Hester, as I was nine years ago? Even then, I was in the autumn of my days, nor was it the early autumn. But all my life had been made up of earnest, studious, thoughtful, quiet years, bestowed faithfully for the increase of my own knowledge, and faithfully, too, though this latter object was but casual to the other,— faithfully for the advancement of human welfare. No life had been more peaceful and innocent than mine; few lives so rich with benefits conferred. Dost thou remember me? Was I not, though you might deem me cold, nevertheless a man thoughtful of others, craving little for himself,— kind, true, just, and of constant, if not warm, affections? Was I not all this?"

"All this, and more," said Hester.

"And what am I now?" demanded he, looking into

her face, and permitting the whole evil within him to be written on his features. "I have already told thee what I am! A fiend! Who made me so?"

"It was myself!" cried Hester, shuddering. "It was I, not less than he. Why hast thou not avenged thyself on me?"

"I have left thee to the scarlet letter," replied Roger Chillingworth. "If that has not avenged me, I can do no more!"

He laid his finger on it, with a smile.

"It has avenged thee!" answered Hester Prynne.

"I judged no less," said the physician. "And now, what wouldst thou with me touching this man?"

"I must reveal the secret," answered Hester, firmly. "He must see thee in thy true character. What may be the result, I know not. But this long debt of confidence, due from me to him, whose ruin I have been, shall at last be paid. So far as concerns the overthrow or preservation of his fair fame and his earthly state, and perhaps his life, he is in thy hands. Nor do I,—whom the scarlet letter has disciplined to truth, though it be the truth of red-hot iron, entering into the soul,—nor do I see such advantage in *his* living any longer a life of ghastly emptiness, that I shall stoop to implore thy mercy. Do with him as thou wilt! There is no good for him,—no good for me,—no good for thee! There is no good for little Pearl! There is no path to guide us out of this dismal maze!"

"Woman, I could almost pity thee!" said Roger Chillingworth, unable to restrain a thrill of admiration too; for there was a quality almost majestic in her despair. "Thou hadst great elements. Perhaps, hadst thou met earlier with a better love than mine, this evil had not been. I pity you, for the good that has been wasted in your nature!"

"And I you," answered Hester Prynne, "for the hatred that has transformed a wise and just man into a fiend!

Wilt thou yet purge it out of thee, and be once more human? If not for his sake, then doubly for your own! Forgive, and leave his further retribution to the Power that claims it! I said, but now, that there could be no good event for *him,* or *thee,* or *me,* who are here wandering together in this gloomy maze of evil, and stumbling, at every step, over the guilt wherewith we have strewn our path. It is not so! There might be good for thee, and thee alone, since thou hast been deeply wronged, and hast it at thy will to pardon. Will you give up that only privilege? Will you reject that priceless benefit!

"Peace, Hester, peace!" replied the old man, with gloomy sternness. "It is not granted *me* to pardon. I have no such power as you speak of. My old faith, long forgotten, comes back to me, and explains all that we do, and all we suffer. By your first step awry you did plant the germ of evil; but since that moment, it has all been a dark necessity. It is our fate. Let the black flower blossom as it may! Now go thy ways, and deal as thou wilt with yonder man."

He waved his hand, and returned to his employment of gathering herbs.

15 *Hester and Pearl*

So Roger Chillingworth—a deformed old figure, with a face that haunted men's memories longer than they liked—took leave of Hester Prynne, and went stooping away along the earth. He gathered here and there an herb, or grubbed up a root, and put it into the basket on his arm. His gray beard almost touched the ground, as he crept onward. Hester gazed after him a little while, looking with a half-fantastic curiosity to see whether the tender grass of early spring would not be blighted beneath him, and show the wavering track of his footsteps, blasted and brown, across its cheerful verdure. She wondered what sort of herbs they were, which the old man was so busy in gathering. Would not the earth, quickened to an evil purpose by the sympathy of his eye, greet him with poisonous shrubs, of species hitherto unknown, that would start up under his fingers?

"Be it sin or no," said Hester Prynne, bitterly, as she still gazed after him, "I hate the man!"

She scolded herself for the sentiment, but could not overcome or lessen it. Attempting to do so, she thought of those long-past days, in a distant land, when he used to emerge at eventide from the seclusion of his study, and sit down in the firelight of their home, and in the light of her wifely smile. He needed to bask himself in that smile, he said, in order that the chill of so many lonely hours among his books might be taken off the scholar's heart. Such scenes had once seemed happy; but now, as viewed through the dismal medium of her later life, they classed themselves among her ugliest remembrances. She marvelled how such scenes could have been! She marvelled how she could ever have been brought to marry him! She deemed it her crime most to be repented of that she had ever endured, and reciprocated, the lukewarm grasp of his hand, and had allowed the smile of her lips and eyes to mingle and melt into his own. And it seemed a fouler offence committed by Roger Chillingworth, than any which had since been done him, that, in the time when her heart knew no better, he had persuaded her to fancy herself happy by his side.

"Yes, I hate him!" repeated Hester, more bitterly than before. "He betrayed me! He has done me worse wrong than I did him!"

The emotions of that brief space, while she stood gazing after the crooked figure of old Roger Chillingworth, threw a dark light on Hester's state of mind, revealing much that she might not otherwise have acknowledged to herself.

He being gone, she summoned back her child.

"Pearl! Pearl! where are you?"

Pearl, whose activity of spirit never flagged, had been at no loss for amusement while her mother talked with the old gatherer of herbs. At first, as already told, she had flirted fancifully with her own image in a pool of water, beckoning the phantom forth, and seeking a passage for herself into its sphere of unreal earth and unattainable sky. Soon finding, however, that either she or the image was unreal, she turned elsewhere for better pastime. She made little boats out of birch-bark, and freighted them with snail-shells, and sent out more ventures on the mighty deep than any merchant in New England; but the larger part of them foundered near the shore. She seized a live horse-shoe crab by the tail, made prize of several five-fingers, and laid out a jellyfish to melt in the warm sun. Then she took up the white foam, that streaked the line of the advancing tide, and threw it upon the breeze, scampering after it, with winged footsteps, to catch the great snow-flakes as they fell. Perceiving a flock of beach-birds, that fed and fluttered along the shore, the naughty child picked up her apron full of pebbles, and creeping from rock to rock after these small sea-fowl, displayed remarkable skill in pelting them. One little gray bird, with a white breast, Pearl was almost sure, had been hit by a pebble, and fluttered away with a broken wing. But then the elf-child sighed, and gave up her sport; because it grieved her to have done harm to a little being that was as wild as the sea-breeze, or as wild as Pearl herself.

Her final employment was to gather seaweed, of various kinds, and make herself a scarf, or mantle, and a headdress, and thus take on the appearance of a little mermaid. She inherited her mother's gift for devising drapery and costume. As the last touch to her mermaid's garb, Pearl took some eel-grass, and imitated, as best she could, on her own bosom, the decoration which she knew so well on her mother's. A letter,—the letter A,—but green, instead of scarlet! The child bent her chin upon her breast, and looked at this device with strange interest; even as if the one and only thing for which she had been sent into the world was to make out its hidden meaning.

"I wonder if mother will ask me what it means!" thought Pearl.

Just then, she heard her mother's voice, and flitting along as lightly as one of the little sea-birds, appeared before Hester Prynne, dancing, laughing, and pointing her finger to the ornament.

"My little Pearl," said Hester, after a moment's silence, "the green letter, and on thy childish bosom, has no meaning. But dost thou know, my child, what this letter means which thy mother is doomed to wear?"

"Yes, mother," said the child. "It is the large letter A. Thou has taught me in the horn-book."[1]

Hester looked steadily into her little face; but, though there was that strange expression which she had so often remarked in her black eyes, she could not satisfy herself whether Pearl really attached any meaning to the symbol. She felt a morbid desire to find out.

"Dost thou know, child, why thy mother wears this letter?"

"Truly do I!" answered Pearl, looking brightly into her mother's face. "It is for the same reason that the minister keeps his hand over his heart!"

"And what reason is that?" asked Hester, half smiling at the child's observation; but, on second thoughts, turning pale. "What has the letter to do with any heart, save mine?"

"Nay, mother, I have told all I know," said Pearl, more seriously than she was in the habit of speaking. "Ask yonder old man whom thou hast been talking with! It may be he can tell. But in good earnest now, mother dear, what does this scarlet letter mean?—and why dost thou wear it on thy bosom?—and why does the minister keep his hand over his heart?"

"What shall I say?" said Hester to herself. "No! If this be the price of the child's sympathy, I cannot pay it."

Then she spoke aloud.

"Silly Pearl, what questions are these? There are many things in this world that a child must not ask about. What know *I* of the minister's heart? And as for the scarlet letter, I wear it for the sake of its gold-thread."

[1] horn-book: a child's book used in colonial days, each page of which was covered with transparent horn and was set in a frame

In all the seven bygone years, Hester Prynne had never before been false to the symbol on her bosom. It may be that it was the charm of a stern and severe, but yet a guardian spirit, who now forsook her; as recognizing that, in spite of his strict watch over her heart, some new evil had crept into it, or some old one had never been expelled. As for little Pearl, the earnestness soon passed out of her face.

But the child did not let the matter drop. Two or three times, as her mother and she went homeward, and as often at supper-time, and while Hester was putting her to bed, and once after she seemed to be fairly asleep, Pearl looked up, with mischief gleaming in her black eyes.

"Mother," said she, "what does the scarlet letter mean?"

And the next morning, the first sign the child gave of being awake was by popping up her head from the pillow, and making that other inquiry, which she had so unaccountably connected with the scarlet letter,—

"Mother!—Mother!—Why does the minister keep his hand over his heart?"

"Hold thy tongue, naughty child!" answered her mother, with a severity that she had never permitted to herself before. "Do not tease me, else I shall shut thee into the dark closet!"

16 *A Forest Walk*

Hester Prynne remained constant in her resolve to make known to the clergyman, at whatever risk of present pain or consequences, the true character of the man who had crept into his intimacy. For several days, however, she vainly sought an opportunity of addressing him in some of the walks which she knew him to be in the habit of taking, along the shores of the peninsula, or on the wooded hills of the neighboring country. There would have been no scandal, indeed, nor peril to the holy whiteness of his good fame, had she visited him in his own study, where many a penitent, ere now, had confessed sins of perhaps as deep a dye as the one betokened by the scarlet letter. But, partly that she dreaded the secret or undisguised interference of old Roger Chillingworth, and partly that her conscious heart imputed suspicion where none could have been felt, and partly that both the minister and she would need the whole wide world to breathe in, while they talked together,—for all these reasons, Hester never thought of meeting him in any narrower privacy than beneath the open sky.

At last, while attending in a sick-chamber, whither the minister had been summoned to make a prayer, she learnt that he had gone, the day before, to visit the Apostle Eliot,[1]

[1] Apostle Eliot: John Eliot, the "Apostle of the Indians"

among his Indian converts. He would probably return, by a certain hour, in the afternoon of the morrow. Early therefore, the next day, Hester took little Pearl,—who was necessarily the companion of all her mother's expeditions, however inconvenient her presence,—and set forth.

The road, after the two wayfarers had crossed from the peninsula to the mainland, was no other than a footpath. It straggled onward into the mystery of the primeval forest. This hemmed it in narrowly, and stood black and dense on either side, and disclosed imperfect glimpses of the sky above. The day was chill and sombre. Overhead was a gray expanse of cloud, slightly stirred, however, by a breeze; so that a gleam of flickering sunshine might now and then be seen at its solitary play along the path. This flitting cheerfulness was always at the farther extremity of some long vista through the forest. The sportive sunlight withdrew itself as they came near, and left the spots where it had danced the drearier, because they had hoped to find them bright.

"Mother," said little Pearl, "the sunshine does not love you. It runs away and hides itself, because it is afraid of something on your bosom. Now see! There it is, playing, a good way off. Stand you here, and let me run and catch it. I am but a child. It will not flee from me, for I wear nothing on my bosom yet!"

"Nor ever will, my child, I hope," said Hester.

"And why not, mother?" asked Pearl, stopping short, just at the beginning of her race. "Will not it come of its own accord, when I am a woman grown?"

"Run away, child," answered her mother, "and catch the sunshine! It will soon be gone."

Pearl set forth, at a great pace, and, as Hester smiled to perceive, actually caught the sunshine, and stood laughing in the midst of it, all brightened by its splendor. The light lingered about the lovely child, as if glad of such a

playmate, until her mother had drawn almost near enough
to step into the magic circle too.

"It will go now," said Pearl, shaking her head.

"See!" answered Hester, smiling. "Now I can stretch
out my hand, and grasp some of it."

As she attempted to do so, the sunshine vanished; or,
to judge from the bright expression that was dancing on
Pearl's features, her mother could have fancied that the
child had absorbed it into herself, and would give it forth
again, with a gleam about her path, as they should plunge
into some gloomier shade. There was no other attribute
that so much impressed her with a sense of new and
untransmitted vigor in Pearl's nature, as this never-failing

vivacity of spirits; she had not the disease of sadness, which almost all children, in these latter days, inherit, with other ills, from the troubles of their ancestors. Perhaps this too was a disease, and but the reflex of the wild energy with which Hester had fought against her sorrows before Pearl's birth.

"Come, my child!" said Hester, looking about her from the spot where Pearl had stood still in the sunshine. "We will sit down a little way within the wood, and rest."

"I am not weary, mother," replied the little girl. "But you may sit down, if you will tell me a story meanwhile."

"A story, child!" said Hester. "And about what?"

"Oh, a story about the Black Man," answered Pearl, taking hold of her mother's gown, and looking up, half earnestly, half mischievously, into her face. "How he haunts this forest, and carries a book with him,—a big, heavy book, with iron clasps; and how this ugly Black Man offers his book and an iron pen to everybody that meets him here among the threes; and they are to write their own names with their own blood. And then he sets his mark on their bosoms! Didst thou ever meet the Black Man, mother?"

"And who told you this story, Pearl?" asked Hester, recognizing a common superstition of the time.

"It was the old dame in the chimney-corner, at the house where you watched last night," said the child. "But she thought me asleep while she was talking of it. She said that thousands of people had met him here, and had written in his book, and have his mark on them. And that ugly-tempered lady, old Mistress Hibbins, was one. And, mother, that old dame said that this scarlet letter was the Black Man's mark on thee, and that it glows like a red flame when you meet him at midnight, here in the dark wood. Is it true, mother? And do you go to meet him in the nighttime?"

"Did you ever awake, and find your mother gone?" asked Hester.

"Not that I remember," said the child. "If you fear to leave me in our cottage, you might take me along. I would gladly go! But mother, tell me! Is there such a Black Man? And didst thou ever meet him? And is this his mark?"

"Wilt thou let me be at peace, if I once tell thee?" asked her mother.

"Yes, if you tell me all," answered Pearl.

"Once in my life I met the Black Man!" said her mother. "This scarlet letter is his mark!"

Thus conversing, they entered sufficiently deep into the wood to secure themselves from the observation of any casual passenger along the forest track. Here they sat down on a luxuriant heap of moss. It was a little dell where they had seated themselves, with a leaf-strewn bank rising gently on either side, and a brook flowing through the midst, over a bed of fallen and drowned leaves. The trees impending over it had flung down great branches, which choked up the current and compelled it to form eddies and black depths at some points; while, in its swifter and livelier passages, there appeared a channelway of pebbles, and brown sparkling sand. Letting the eyes follow along the course of the stream, they could catch the reflected light from its water, at some short distance within the forest. All these giant trees and boulders of granite seemed intent on making a mystery of the course of this small brook; fearing, perhaps, that, with its never-ceasing talkativeness it should whisper tales out of the heart of the old forest whence it flowed, or mirror its revelations on the smooth surface of a pool. Continually, indeed, as it stole onward, the streamlet kept up a babble, kind, quiet, soothing, but melancholy, like the voice of a young child that was spending its infancy without playfulness, and knew not how to be merry among said acquaintances and events of sombre hue.

"O brook! O foolish and tiresome little brook!" cried Pearl, after listening awhile to its talk. "Why art thou so sad? Pluck up spirit, and do not be all the time sighing and murmuring!"

But the brook, in the course of its little lifetime among the forest-trees, had gone through so solemn an experience that it could not help talking about it, and seemed to have nothing else to say. Pearl resembled the brook, inasmuch as the current of her life gushed from a wellspring as mysterious, and had flowed through scenes shadowed as heavily with gloom. But, unlike the little stream, she danced and sparkled, and prattled airily along her course.

"And what does this sad little brook say, mother?" inquired she.

"If you had a sorrow of your own, the brook might tell you of it," answered her mother, "even as it is telling me of mine! But now, Pearl, I hear a footstep along the paths, and the noise of one putting aside the branches. I would have thee betake thyself to play, and leave me to speak with him that comes yonder."

"Is it the Black Man?" asked Pearl.

"Wilt thou go and play, child?" repeated her mother. "But do not stray far into the wood. And take heed that you come at my first call."

"Yes, mother," answered Pearl. "But if it be the Black Man, wilt thou not let me stay a moment, and look at him, with his big book under his arm?"

"Go, silly child!" said Hester, impatiently. "It is no Black Man! Thou canst see him now, through the trees. It is the minister."

"And so it is!" said the child. "And, mother, he has his hand over his heart! Is it because, when the minister wrote his name in the book, the Black Man set his mark in that place? But why does he not wear it outside his bosom, as thou dost, mother?"

"Go now, child; thou shalt tease me as thou wilt another time," cried Hester Prynne. "But do not stray far. Keep where you can hear the babble of the brook."

When her elf-child had departed, Hester Prynne made a step or two towards the track that led through the forest, but still remained under the deep shadow of the trees. She saw the minister advancing along the path alone, and leaning on a staff which he had cut by the wayside. He looked haggard and feeble. There was a listlessness in his gait; as if he saw no reason for taking one step farther, nor felt any desire to do so, but would have been glad, could he be glad of anything, to fling himself down at the root of the nearest tree, and lie there passive, for evermore.

17 *The Pastor and His Parishioner*

Slowly as the minister walked, he had almost gone by, before Hester Prynne could gather voice enough to call him. At length, she succeeded.

"Arthur Dimmesdale!" she said, faintly at first; then louder. "Arthur Dimmesdale!"

"Who speaks?" asked the minister.

Gathering himself quickly up, he stood more erect, like a man taken by surprise in a mood to which he was reluctant to have witness. Throwing his eyes anxiously in the direction of the voice, he indistinctly beheld a form under the trees, clad in garments so depressing, and so little relieved from the gray twilight into which the clouded sky and the heavy foliage had darkened the noontide, that he knew not whether it were a woman or a shadow.

He came closer, and discovered the scarlet letter.

"Hester! Hester Prynne!" said he. "Is it thou? Art thou in life?"

"Even so!" she answered. "In such life as has been mine these seven years past! And thou, Arthur Dimmesdale, dost thou yet live?"

It was no wonder that they thus questioned one another's actual and bodily existence, and even doubted of their own. So strangely did they meet, in the dim wood, that it was like the first encounter, in the world beyond the grave, of two spirits who had been intimately connected in their former life, but now stood coldly shuddering, in mutual fear; as not yet familiar with their state, nor used to the companionship of disembodied beings. Each a ghost, and awe-stricken at the other ghost! They were awe-stricken likewise at themselves; because the crisis flung back to them their consciousness, and revealed to each heart its history and experience, as life never does, except at such breathless epochs.[1] The soul beheld its features in the mirror of the passing moment. It was with fear, and tremulously, and, as it were, by a slow, reluctant necessity, that Arthur Dimmesdale put forth his hand, cold as death, and touched the chill hand of Hester Prynne. The grasp, cold as it was, took away what was dreariest in the interview. They now felt themselves, at least, inhabitants of the same sphere.

Without a word more spoken, they glided back into the shadow of the woods, whence Hester had emerged, and sat down on the heap of moss where she and Pearl had before been sitting. When they could speak, it was, at first, only to utter remarks and inquiries such as any two acquaintances might have made, about the gloomy sky, the threatening storm, and next, the health of each. Thus they went onward, not boldly, but step by step, into the themes that were brooding deepest in their hearts. So long separated by fate and circumstances, they needed something slight and casual to run before, and throw open the doors of communication, so that their real thoughts might be led across the threshold.

After a while, the minister fixed his eyes on Hester Prynne.

"Hester," said he, "hast thou found peace?"

She smiled drearily, looking down upon her bosom.

"Hast thou?" she asked.

[1] epochs: memorable moments

"None!—nothing but despair!" he answered. "What else could I look for, being what I am, and leading such a life as mine? Were I an atheist, I might have found peace, long ere now. Nay, I never should have lost it! But, as matters stand with my soul, whatever of good there originally was in me, all of God's gifts that were the choicest have become the agents of spiritual torment. Hester, I am most miserable!"

"The people reverence you," said Hester. "And surely thou workest good among them! Does this bring you no comfort?"

"More misery, Hester!—only more misery!" answered the clergyman, with a bitter smile. "As concerns the good which I may appear to do, I have no faith in it. It is a delusion.[2] What can a ruined soul, like mine, effect towards the saving of other souls?—or a polluted soul towards their purification? And as for the people's reverence, would that it were turned to scorn and hatred! Can you deem it, Hester, a consolation, that I must stand up in my pulpit, and meet so many eyes turned upward to my face, as if the light of heaven were beaming from it!—and then look inward, and discern the black reality of what they idolize? I have laughed in bitterness and agony of heart at the contrast between what I seem and what I am! And Satan laughs at it!"

"You wrong yourself in this," said Hester, gently. "You have deeply and sorely repented. Your sin is left behind you, in the days long past. Your present life is not less holy, in very truth, than it seems in people's eyes. Is there no reality in the penitence thus sealed and witnessed by good works? And wherefore should it not bring you peace?"

"No, Hester, no!" replied the clergyman. "There is no substance in it! It is cold and dead, and can do nothing for

[2] delusion: false belief

me! Of penance,[3] I have had enough! Of penitence,[4] there
has been none! Else, I should long ago have thrown off
these garments of mock holiness, and have shown myself
to mankind as they will see me at the judgment-seat.
Happy are you, Hester, wearing the scarlet letter *openly*
upon your bosom! Mine burns in secret! Thou little knowest what a relief it is, after the torment of a seven years'
cheat, to look into a face that recognizes me for what I
am! Had I one friend—or were it my worst enemy!—to
whom, when sickened with the praises of all other men, I
could daily betake myself, and be known as the vilest of
all sinners, methinks my soul might keep itself alive
thereby. Even thus much of truth would save me! But,
now, it is all falsehood!—all emptiness!—all death!"

Hester Prynne looked into his face, but hesitated to
speak. Yet, uttering his long-restrained emotions so vehe-
mently as he did, his words here offered her the very
opportunity in which to say what she came to say. She
conquered her fears, and spoke.

"Such a friend as you have even now wished for," said
she, "with whom to weep over your sin, you have in *me*,
the partner of it!"—Again she hesitated, but brought out
the words with an effort.—"You have long had such an
enemy, and dwell with him,—under the same roof!"

The minister started to his feet, gasping for breath,
and clutching at his heart, as if he would have torn it out
of his bosom.

"Ha! What are you saying!" cried he. "An enemy! And
under mine own roof! What mean you?"

Hester Prynne was now fully sensible of the deep
injury for which she was responsible to this unhappy man,
in permitting him to lie for so many years, or indeed, for a
single moment, at the mercy of one whose purposes could

[3] penance: self-punishment for having sinned
[4] penitence: sincere sorrow for having sinned

not be other than evil. The very closeness of his enemy, beneath whatever mask the latter might conceal himself, was enough to disturb so sensitive a being as Arthur Dimmesdale. There had been a period when Hester was less alive to this consideration; or, perhaps, in her hatred of humanity because of her own trouble, she left the minister to bear what she might think a more tolerable doom. But of late, since the night of his vigil, all her sympathies towards him had been both softened and invigorated. She now read his heart more accurately. She doubted not, that the continual presence of Roger Chillingworth,—the secret poison of his malignity,[5] infecting all the air about him,— and his authorized interference, as a physician, with the minister's physical and spiritual infirmities,—that these bad opportunities had been turned to a cruel purpose. By means of them, the sufferer's conscience had been kept in an irritated state, the tendency of which was, not to cure by wholesome pain, but to disorganize and corrupt his spiritual being. Its result, on earth, could hardly fail to be insanity, and hereafter, that eternal alienation from the Good and True, of which madness is perhaps the earthly type.

Such was the ruin to which she had brought the man, once,—nay, why should we not speak of it?—*still* so

[5] malignity: intense hatred

passionately loved! Hester felt the sacrifice of the clergyman's good name, and death itself, as she had already told
Roger Chillingworth, would have been infinitely preferable
to the alternative which she had taken upon herself to
choose. And now, rather than have had this grievous wrong
to confess, she would gladly have lain down on the forest-
leaves, and died, there, at Arthur Dimmesdale's feet.

"Oh Arthur," cried she, "forgive me! In all things else,
I have striven to be true! Truth was the one virtue which
I might have held fast, and did hold fast, through all extremity; save when thy good,—thy life,—thy fame,—were
put in question! Then I consented to a lie. But a lie is
never good, even though death threaten on the other side!
Dost thou not see what I would say? That old man!—the
physician!—he whom they call Roger Chillingworth!—he
was—my husband!"

The minister looked at her for an instant, with all that
violence of passion, which was, in fact, the portion of him
which the Devil claimed and through which he sought to
win the rest. Never was there a blacker or a fiercer frown
than Hester now saw on his face. For the brief space that
it lasted, it was a dark change. But his character had been
so much enfeebled by suffering, that even its lower energies were incapable of more than a brief struggle. He sank
down on the ground, and buried his face in his hands.

"I might have known it," murmured he. "I did know
it! Was not the secret told me, in the natural recoil of my
heart, at first sight of him, and as often as I have seen him
since? Why did I not understand? Oh Hester Prynne, thou
little, little knowest all the horror of this thing! And the
shame!—the indelicacy!—the horrible ugliness—of this
exposure of a sick and guilty heart to the very eye that
would gloat over it! Woman, woman, you are responsible
for this! I cannot forgive you!"

"Thou shalt forgive me!" cried Hester, flinging herself

on the fallen leaves beside him. "Let God punish! Thou shalt forgive! Thou must!"

With sudden and desperate tenderness, she threw her arms around him, and pressed his head against her bosom; little caring that his cheek rested on the scarlet letter. He would have released himself, but strove in vain to do so. Hester would not set him free, lest he should look her sternly in the face again. All the world had frowned on her,—for seven long years had it frowned upon this lonely woman,—and still she bore it all, nor ever once turned away her firm, sad eyes. But *his* frown, the frown of this pale, weak, sinful, sorrow-stricken man was more than Hester could bear—and live!

"Wilt thou yet forgive me!" she repeated, over and over again. "Wilt thou frown? Wilt thou forgive?"

"Yes, yes, I forgive you, Hester," replied the minister, at length. "I freely forgive you now. May God forgive us both! We are not, Hester, the worst sinners in the world. There is one far worse than even the polluted priest! That old man's revenge has been blacker than my sin. He has violated, in cold blood, the sanctity of a human heart. Thou and I, Hester, never did so!"

"Never, never!" whispered she. "What we did had a consecration of its own. We felt it so! We said so to each other! Hast thou forgotten it?"

"Hush, Hester!" said Arthur Dimmesdale, rising from the ground. "No; I have not forgotten!"

They sat down again, side by side, and hand clasped in hand, on the mossy trunk of the fallen tree. Life had never brought them a gloomier hour; it was the point whither their pathway had so long been tending, and darkening ever, as it stole along; and yet it enclosed a charm that made them linger upon it, and claim another, and another, and, after all, another moment. The forest was obscure around them, and creaked with a blast that was passing through it. The boughs were tossing heavily above their heads; while one solemn old tree groaned sadly to another, as if telling the sad story of the pair that sat beneath, or forced to forebode evil to come.

And still they lingered. How dreary looked the forest-track that led backward to the settlement, where Hester Prynne must take up again the burden of her disgrace, and the minister the hollow mockery of his good name! So they lingered an instant longer. No golden light had ever been so precious as the gloom of this dark forest. Here, seen only by *his* eyes, the scarlet letter need not burn into the bosom of the fallen woman! Here, seen only by *her* eyes, Arthur Dimmesdale, false to God and man, might be, for one moment, true—to himself and to her!

He started at a thought that suddenly struck him.

"Hester," cried he, "here is a new horror! Roger Chillingworth knows your purpose to reveal his true character. Will he continue, then, to keep our secret? What will now be the course of his revenge?"

"There is a strange secrecy in his nature," replied Hester, "and it has grown upon him by the hidden practices of his revenge. I do not think that he will betray our secret. He will doubtless seek other means of indulging his dark passion."

"And I!—how can I live longer, breathing the same air as this deadly enemy?" exclaimed Arthur Dimmesdale, shrinking within himself, and pressing his hand to his heart,—a gesture that had grown involuntary with him. "Think of me, Hester! Thou art strong. Decide for me!"

"Thou must dwell no longer with this man," said Hester, slowly and firmly. "Thy heart must be no longer under his evil eye!"

"It were far worse than death!" replied the minister. "But how to avoid it? What choice remains to me? Shall I lie down again on these withered leaves, where I cast myself when you told me what he was? Must I sink down there, and die at once?"

"Alas, what a ruin has befallen thee!" said Hester, with tears in her eyes. "Wilt thou die for very weakness? There is no other cause!"

"The judgment of God is on me," answered the conscience-stricken priest. "It is too mighty for me to struggle with!"

"Heaven would show mercy," rejoined Hester, "hadst thou but the strength to take advantage of it."

"Be strong for me!" answered he. "What am I to do!"

"Is the world, then, so narrow?" exclaimed Hester Prynne, fixing her deep eyes on the minister's and instinctively exercising a magnetic power over a spirit so shattered and subdued that it could hardly hold itself erect. "Doth the universe lie within the compass of yonder town, which only a little time ago was but a leaf-strewn desert, as lonely as this around us? Whither leads yonder forest-track? Backward to the settlement, thou sayest! Yes; but onward, too. Deeper it goes, and deeper, into the wilderness, less plainly to be seen at every step until, some few miles hence the yellow leaves will show no trace of the white man's tread. There thou art free! So brief a journey would bring you from a world where you have been most wretched, to one where you may still be happy! Is there not shade enough in all this boundless forest to hide your heart from the gaze of Roger Chillingworth?"

"Yes, Hester; but only under the fallen leaves!" replied the minister, with a sad smile.

"Then there is the broad pathway of the sea!" continued Hester. "It brought thee hither. If thou so choose, it will bear thee back again. In our native land, whether in some remote rural village or in vast London,—or in Germany, in France, in pleasant Italy,—thou wouldst be beyond his power and knowledge!"

"It cannot be!" answered the minister. "I am powerless to go! Wretched and sinful as I am, I have had no other thought than to drag on my earthly existence in the sphere where Providence hath placed me. Lost as my soul is, I would still do what I may for other souls! I dare not quit my post, though an unfaithful sentinel, whose sure reward is death and dishonor, when his dreary watch shall come to an end!"

"Thou art crushed under this seven years' weight of misery," replied Hester. "Leave this wreck and ruin here where it hath happened. Meddle no more with it! Begin all anew! Hast thou exhausted possibility in the failure of this one trial? Not so! The future is yet full of trial and success. There is happiness to be enjoyed! There is good to be done! Exchange this false life for a true one. Be, if thy spirit summon thee to such a mission, the teacher and apostle of the red men. Or,—as is more thy nature,—be a scholar and a sage among the wisest and most renowned of the cultivated world. Preach! Write! Act! Do something, *anything*, except to lie down and die! Give up your name of Arthur Dimmesdale, and make yourself another, and a high one, such as you can wear without fear or shame. Why shouldst thou tarry so much as one more day in the torments that have so gnawed into thy life!—that have made thee feeble to will and to do!—that will leave thee powerless even to repent! Up, and away!"

"Oh Hester!" cried Arthur Dimmesdale, in whose eyes a fitful light, kindled by her enthusiasm, flashed up and then died down, "thou tellest of running a race to a man whose knees are tottering beneath him! I must die here! There is not the strength or courage left me to venture into the wide, strange, difficult world, alone!"

It was the last expression of the despair of a broken spirit. He lacked energy to grasp the better fortune that seemed within his reach.

He repeated the word.

"Alone, Hester! Alone!"

"Thou shalt not go alone!" answered she, in a deep whisper. "Not alone!"

Then, all was spoken!—all, in one word!

18 *A Flood of Sunshine*

Arthur Dimmesdale gazed into Hester's face with a look in which hope and joy shone out, indeed, but with fear and a kind of horror at her boldness, who had spoken what he vaguely hinted at but dared not speak.

But Hester Prynne, with a mind of native courage and activity, and for so long a period not merely estranged, but outlawed, from society, had habituated herself to such freedom of thought as was altogether foreign to the clergyman. She had wandered, without rule or guidance, in moral wilderness; as vast, as intricate and shadowy, as the untamed forest, amid the gloom of which they were now holding a conference that was to decide their fate. Her intellect and heart had their home, as it were, in desert places, where she roamed as freely as the wild Indian in his woods. For years past she had looked from this estranged point of view at human institutions, and whatever priests or legislators had established; criticizing all with hardly more reverence than the Indian would feel for the clerical band, the judicial robe, the pillory, the gallows, the fireside, or the church. The tendency of her fate and fortunes had been to set her free. The scarlet letter was her passport into regions where other women dared not tread. Shame, Despair, Solitude! These had been her teachers,— stern and wild ones,—and they had made her strong.

The minister, on the other hand, had never gone through an experience calculated to lead him beyond the scope of generally accepted laws; although, in a single instance, he had so fearfully broken one of the most sacred of them. But this had been a sin of passion, not of principle, nor even purpose. Since that wretched epoch, he had watched, with morbid zeal and minuteness, not his acts,— for those it was easy to arrange,—but each breath of emotion, and his every thought. At the head of the social system, as the clergymen of that day stood, he was only the more chained by its regulations, its principles, and even its prejudices. As a priest, the framework of his order inevitably hemmed him in. As a man who had once sinned, but who kept his conscience all alive and painfully sensitive by the chafing of an unhealed wound, he might have been supposed safer within the line of virtue than if he had never sinned at all.

Thus, as regarded Hester Prynne, the whole seven years of outlaw and shame had been little more than a preparation for this very hour. But Arthur Dimmesdale! Were such a man once more to fall, what plea could be urged to excuse his crime? None; unless it avail him somewhat, that he was broken down by long and intense suffering; that his mind was darkened and confused by the very remorse which harrowed it; that between fleeing as an avowed criminal, and remaining as a hypocrite, conscience might find it hard to strike the balance, that it was human to avoid the peril of death and infamy, the inscrutable machinations[1] of an enemy; that, finally, to this poor pilgrim, on his dreary and desert path, faint, sick, miserable, there appeared a glimpse of human affection and sympathy, a new life, and a true one, in exchange for the heavy doom which he was now expiating. And be the stern and sad truth spoken, that the breach which guilt has once

[1] inscrutable machinations: mysterious and hostile plotting

made into the human soul is never, in this mortal state, repaired.

The struggle, if it were one, need not be described. Let it suffice, that the clergyman resolved to flee, and not alone.

"If, in all these past seven years" thought he, "I could recall one instant of peace or hope, I would yet endure for the sake of that promise of Heaven's mercy. But now,— since I am irrevocably[2] doomed,—why should I not snatch the comfort allowed to the criminal before his execution? Of, if this be the path to a better life, as Hester would persuade me, I surely give up no fairer prospect by pursuing it! Neither can I any longer live without her companionship; so powerful is she to sustain,—so tender to soothe! O Thou to whom I dare not lift mine eyes, wilt Thou yet pardon me!"

"Thou wilt go!" said Hester, calmly, as he met her glance.

The decision once made, a glow of strange enjoyment threw its flickering brightness over the trouble of his breast. It was the stimulating effect—upon a prisoner just escaped from the dungeon of his own heart—of breathing the wild, free atmosphere of an unredeemed, lawless region. His spirit rose, as it were, with a bound, and attained a nearer prospect of the sky, than throughout all the misery which had kept him grovelling on the earth.

"Do I feel joy again?" cried he, wondering at himself. "I thought the germ of it was dead in me! Oh Hester, thou art my better angel! I seem to have flung myself—sick, sin-stained, and sorrow-blackened—down upon these forest-leaves, and to have risen up all made anew, and with new powers to glorify Him that hath been merciful! This is already the better life! Why did we not find it sooner?"

"Let us not look back," answered Hester Prynne. "The

[2] irrevocably: with no possibility of change

past is gone! Why should we linger upon it now? See! With this symbol, I undo it all, and make it as if it had never been!"

So speaking, she undid the clasp that fastened the scarlet letter, and, taking it from her bosom, threw it among the withered leaves. The mystic token alighted on the nearer edge of the stream. With a hand's breadth farther flight it would have fallen into the water, and have given the little brook another woe to carry onward, besides the unintelligible tale which it still kept murmuring about. But there lay the embroidered letter, glittering like a lost jewel, which some ill-fated wanderer might pick up, and thenceforth be haunted by strange phantoms of guilt, sinkings of the heart, and unaccountable misfortune.

The sign of shame gone, Hester heaved a long, deep sigh, in which the burden of anguish departed from her spirit. Oh exquisite relief! She had not known the weight, until she felt the freedom! By another impulse, she took off the formal cap that bound her hair; and down it fell upon her shoulders, dark, rich, with a shadow and a light in its abundance, and imparting a charm of softness to her features. There played around her mouth, and beamed out of her eyes, a radiant and tender smile, that seemed gushing from the very heart of womanhood. A crimson flush was glowing on her cheek, that had been long so pale. Her sex, her youth, and the whole richness of her beauty, came back from the irrevocable past, and clustered themselves, with her maiden hope, and a happiness before unknown, within the magic circle of this hour. All at once, as with a sudden smile of heaven, forth burst the sunshine, pouring a very flood into the obscure forest, gladdening each green leaf, transmuting the yellow fallen ones to gold, and gleaming adown the gray trunks of the solemn trees. The objects that had made a shadow hitherto, embodied the brightness now. The course of the little brook might be traced by its

merry gleam afar into the wood's heart of mystery, which had become a mystery of joy.

Such was the sympathy of Nature—that wild, heathen Nature of the forest, never subjugated by human law, nor illumined by higher truth—with the bliss of these two spirits! Love, whether newly born, or aroused from a death-like slumber, must always create a sunshine, filling the heart so full of radiance, that it overflows upon the outward world. Had the forest still kept its gloom, it would have been bright in Hester's eyes, and bright in Arthur Dimmesdale's!

Hester looked at him with the thrill of another joy.

"You must know Pearl!" said she. "Our little Pearl! You have seen her,—yes, I know it!—but you will see her now with other eyes. She is a strange child! I hardly comprehend her! But you will love her dearly, as I do, and will advise me how to deal with her."

"Do you think she will be glad to know me?" asked the minister, somewhat uneasily. "I have long shrunk from children, because they often show a distrust,—a backwardness—to be familiar with me. I have even been afraid of little Pearl!"

"Ah, that was sad!" answered the mother. "But she will love you dearly, and you her. She is not far off. I will call her! Pearl! Pearl!"

"I see her," said the minister. "Yonder she is, standing in a streak of sunshine, a good way off, on the other side of the brook. So you think the child will love me?"

Hester smiled, and again called to Pearl, who was visible, at some distance, as the minister had described her, like a bright-apparelled vision, in a sunbeam, which fell down upon her through an arch of boughs. The ray quivered to and fro, making her figure dim or distinct,— now like a real child, now like a child's spirit,—as the splendor went and came again. She heard her mother's voice, and approached slowly through the forest.

Pearl had not found the hour pass wearisomely, while her mother sat talking with the clergyman. The great black forest—stern as it showed itself to those who brought the guilt and troubles of the world into its bosom—became the playmate of the lonely infant, as well as it knew how. Sombre as it was, it put on its kindest mood to welcome her. It offered her the partridge-berries, the growth of the preceding autumn, but ripening only in the spring, and now red as drops of blood upon the withered leaves. These Pearl gathered, pleased with their wild flavor. The small inhabitants of the wilderness hardly took pains to move out of her path. A partridge indeed, with a brood of ten behind her, ran forward threateningly, but soon repented of her fierceness, and clucked to her young ones not to be afraid. A pigeon, alone on a low branch, allowed Pearl to come beneath, and uttered a sound as much of greeting as alarm. A fox, startled from his sleep by her light footstep on the leaves, looked inquisitively at Pearl, as doubting whether it were better to steal off, or continue his nap on the same spot. A wolf, it is said,—but here the tale has surely lapsed into the improbable,—came up, and smelt

Pearl's robe, and offered his savage head to be patted. The truth *seems* to be, however that the mother-forest, and these wild things which it nourished, all recognized a kindred wildness in the human child.

And she was gentler here than in the grassy-margined streets of the settlement, or in her mother's cottage. The flowers appeared to know it; and one and another whispered as she passed, "Adorn thyself with me, beautiful child, adorn thyself with me!"—and, to please them, Pearl gathered the violets, and anemones, and columbines, and some twigs of the freshest green, which the old trees held down before her eyes. With these she decorated her hair, and became a nymph-child, or an infant dryad,[3] or whatever else was in closest sympathy with the antique wood. In such guise had Pearl adorned herself, when she heard her mother's voice, and came slowly back.

Slowly; for she saw the clergyman.

---

[3] dryad: in Greek mythology, a wood-nymph who lived in a tree and died when the tree died

19 *The Child at the Brook-Side*

"You will love her dearly," repeated Hester Prynne, as she and the minister sat watching little Pearl. "Is she not beautiful? And see with what natural skill she has made those simple flowers adorn her! Had she gathered pearls, and diamonds, and rubies, in the wood, they could not have become her better. She is a splendid child! But I now whose brow she has!"

"Dost thou know, Hester," said Arthur Dimmesdale, with an unquiet smile, "that this dear child, tripping about always at thy side, hath caused me much alarm? Methought—Oh Hester, what a thought, and how terrible to dread it!—that my own features were partly reproduced in her face, and so strikingly that the world might see them! But she is mostly thine!"

"No, no! Not mostly!" answered the mother, with a tender smile. "A little longer, and you need not to be afraid to trace whose child she is. But how strangely beautiful she looks, with those wild flowers in her hair! It is as if one of the fairies, whom we left in our dear old England, had decked her out to meet us."

It was with a feeling which neither of them had ever before experienced that they sat and watched Pearl's slow approach. In her was visible the tie that united them.

"Let me see nothing strange—no passion nor any

eagerness—in the way of addressing her," whispered Hester. "Our Pearl is a fitful and fantastic little elf, sometimes. She is seldom tolerant of emotion, when she does not fully comprehend the why and wherefore. But the child has strong affections! She loves me, and will love you!"

"Thou canst not think," said the minister, glancing aside at Hester Prynne, "how my heart dreads this meeting, and yearns for it! But, in truth, as I already told thee, children are not readily won to be friendly with me. They do not climb my knee, nor prattle in my ear, nor answer to my smile; but stand apart, and eye me strangely. Even little babes, when I take them in my arms, weep bitterly. Yet, twice in her little lifetime, Pearl has been kind to me! The first time,—thou knowest it well! The last was when thou ledst her with thee to the house of yonder stern old Governor."

"And thou didst plead so bravely in her behalf and mine!" answered the mother. "I remember it; and so shall little Pearl. Fear nothing! She may be distant and shy at first, but will soon learn to love thee!"

By this time Pearl had reached the margin of the brook, and stood on the farther side, gazing silently at Hester and the clergyman, who still sat together on the mossy tree-trunk, waiting to receive her. Just where she had paused, the brook chanced to form a pool, so smooth and quiet that it reflected a perfect image of her little figure, with all the brilliant picturesqueness of her beauty, in its adornment of flowers and wreathed foliage, but more refined and spiritualized than the reality. This image, so nearly identical with the living Pearl, seemed to communicate somewhat of its own shadowy quality to the child herself. It was strange, the way in which Pearl stood, looking so steadfastly at them through the dim medium of the forest-gloom; herself, meanwhile, all glorified with a ray of sunshine that was attracted thitherward as by a certain sympathy. In the brook beneath stood another child,—another and the same,—with likewise its ray of golden light. Hester felt herself, in some indistinct and tantalizing manner, separated from Pearl; as if the child, in her lonely ramble through the forest, had strayed out of the sphere in which she and her mother dwelt together, and was now vainly seeking to return to it.

There was both truth and error in the impression; the child and mother were estranged,[1] but through Hester's fault, not Pearl's. Since the latter rambled from her side, another member had been admitted within the circle of the mother's feelings, and so modified the aspect of them all, that Pearl, the returning wanderer, could not find her accustomed place, and hardly knew where she was.

"I have a strange fancy," observed the sensitive minister, "that this brook is the boundary between two worlds, and that thou canst never meet thy Pearl again. Or is she an elfish spirit, who is forbidden to cross a running stream? Pray hasten her; for this delay has already imparted a tremor to my nerves."

"Come, dearest child!" said Hester, encouragingly, stretching out her arms. "How slow thou art! When hast thou been so sluggish before? Here is a friend of mine, who must be thy friend also. Thou wilt have twice as much love, henceforward, as thy mother alone could give thee! Leap across the brook, and come to us. Thou canst leap like a young deer!"

Pearl, without responding to these honey-sweet expressions, remained on the other side of the brook. Now she fixed her bright, wild eyes on her mother, now on the minister, and now included them both in the same glance; as if to detect and explain to herself the relationship which they bore to one another. For some unaccountable reason, as Arthur Dimmesdale felt the child's eyes upon him, his

[1] estranged: less close emotionally

hand—with that gesture so habitual as to have become unconscious—stole over his heart. At length, assuming a strange air of authority, Pearl stretched out her hand, with the small forefinger extended, and pointing evidently towards her mother's breast. And beneath, in the mirror of the brook, there was the flower-girdled and sunny image of little Pearl, pointing her small forefinger too.

"Thou strange child, why dost thou not come to me?" exclaimed Hester.

Pearl still pointed with her finger; and a frown gathered on her brow; the more impressive from the childish, almost baby-like aspect of the features that conveyed it. As her mother still kept beckoning to her, and smiling, the child stamped her foot with a yet more imperious look and gesture. In the brook, again, was the fantastic beauty of the image, with its reflected frown, its pointed finger, and imperious gesture, giving emphasis to the aspect of little Pearl.

"Hasten, Pearl; or I shall be angry with thee!" said Hester Prynne, who, however used to such behavior on the elf-child's part at other times, was naturally anxious for a more proper deportment now. "Leap across the brook, naughty child, and run hither! Else I must come to thee!"

But Pearl, not a bit startled at her mother's threats any more than softened by her entreaties, now suddenly burst into a fit of passion, gesticulating violently and throwing her small figure into the most extravagant contortions. She accompanied this wild outbreak with piercing shrieks, which the woods echoed on all sides. Seen in the brook, once more, was the shadowy wrath of Pearl's image, crowned with flowers, but stamping its foot, wildly gesticulating, and, in the midst of all, still pointing its finger at Hester's bosom!

"I see what ails the child," whispered Hester to the clergyman, and turning pale in spite of a strong effort to

conceal her trouble and annoyance. "Children will not abide any, even the slightest, change in the accustomed aspect of things that are daily before their eyes. Pearl misses something which she has always seen me wear!"

"I pray you," answered the minister, "if you have any means of pacifying the child, do it immediately! I know nothing that I would not sooner encounter than this passion in a child. In Pearl's young beauty, as in the wrinkled witch, it has an uncommon effect. Do pacify her, if you love me!"

Hester turned again towards Pearl, with a crimson blush upon her cheek, a conscious glance aside at the clergyman, and then a heavy sigh; while, even before she had time to speak, the blush yielded to a deadly pallor.

"Pearl," said she sadly, "look down at thy feet! There!—before thee!—on the nearer side of the brook!"

The child turned her eyes to the point indicated; and there lay the scarlet letter, so close upon the margin of the stream, that the gold embroidery was reflected in it.

"Bring it hither!" said Hester.

"Come *thou* and take it up!" answered Pearl.

"Was ever such a child!" observed Hester, aside to the minister. "Oh, I have much to tell thee about her! But, in very truth, she is right as regards this hateful token. I must bear its torture a little longer,—only a few days longer,—until we have left this region and look back hither as to a land which we dreamed of. The forest cannot hide it! The mid-ocean shall take it from my hand, and swallow it up forever!"

With these words, she advanced to the margin of the brook, took up the scarlet letter, and fastened it again on her bosom. Hopefully, but a moment ago, as Hester had spoken of drowning it in the deep sea, there was a sense of inevitable doom upon her, as she thus received back this deadly symbol from the hand of fate. She had flung it into infinite space!—she had drawn an hour's free breath!—and here again was the scarlet misery, glittering on the old spot! Hester next gathered up the heavy tresses of her hair, and confined them beneath her cap. As if there were a withering spell in the sad letter, her beauty, her warmth and the richness of her womanhood, departed, like fading sunshine; and a shadow seemed to fall across her.

When the dreary change was made, she extended her hand to Pearl.

"Dost thou know thy mother now, child?" asked she, reproachfully, in a subdued tone. "Wilt thou come across the brook, and own thy mother, now that she has her shame upon her,—now that she is sad?"

"Yes; now I will!" answered the child, bounding across the brook, and clasping Hester in her arms. "Now you are my mother indeed! And I am your little Pearl!"

In a mood of tenderness not unusual with her, she drew down her mother's head, and kissed her brow and both her cheeks. But then—by a kind of necessity that always impelled this child to spoil whatever comfort she might chance to give with a throb of anguish—Pearl put up her mouth, and kissed the scarlet letter too!

"That was not kind!" said Hester. "When thou hast shown me a little love, thou mockest me!"

"Why doth the minister sit yonder?" asked Pearl.

"He waits to welcome you," replied her mother. "Come and beg his blessing! He loves you, my little Pearl, and loves your mother too. Will you not love him? Come! he longs to greet you!"

"Does he love us?" said Pearl, looking up into her mother's face. "Will he go back with us, hand in hand, we three together, into the town?"

"Not now, my dear child," answered Hester. "But in days to come, he will walk hand in hand with us. We will have a home and fireside of our own; and thou shalt sit upon his knee; and he will teach thee many things, and love thee dearly. Thou wilt love him; wilt thou not?"

"And will he always keep his hand over his heart?" inquired Pearl, not answering her mother's query.

"Foolish child, what a question is that!" exclaimed Hester. "Come and ask his blessing!"

But, whether influenced by the jealousy that seems instinctive with every petted child towards a dangerous rival, or from whatever caprice of her freakish nature, Pearl would show no favor to the minister. It was only by an exertion of force that her mother brought her up to him, hanging back, and manifesting her reluctance by odd grimaces; of which, ever since babyhood, she had possessed a singular variety. The minister—painfully embarrassed, but hoping that a kiss might prove a charm to admit him into the child's kindlier regards—bent forward, and impressed one on her brow. Hereupon, Pearl broke away from her mother, and running to the brook, stooped over it, and bathed her forehead, until the unwelcome kiss was quite washed off, and diffused through a long lapse of the gliding water. She then remained apart, silently watching Hester and the clergyman; while they talked together, and made such arrangements as were suggested by their new position, and the purposes soon to be fulfilled.

20 The Minister in a Maze

As the minister departed, in advance of Hester Prynne and little Pearl, he threw a backward glance, half expecting to discover only some faintly traced features or outline of the mother and the child slowly fading into the twilight of the woods. So great a change in his life could not at once be received as real. But there was Hester, clad in her gray robe, still standing beside the tree-trunk, which some blast had overthrown long ago, and which time had ever since been covering with moss, so that these two fated ones, with earth's heaviest burden on them, might there sit down together, and find a single hour's rest and solace. And there was Pearl, too, lightly dancing from the margin of the brook,—now that he, the intrusive third person, was gone,—and taking her old place by her mother's side. So the minister had not fallen asleep and dreamed!

In order to free his mind from this indistinctness and duplicity of impression, which vexed it with a strange disquietude, he recalled and more thoroughly defined the plans which they had sketched for their departure. It had been decided that the Old World, with its crowds and cities, offered them a better shelter than did the wilds of New England, or all America, with its alternatives of Indian wigwams, or the few settlements of Europeans, scattered thinly along the seaboard. Not to speak of the clergyman's health, so unable to sustain the hardships of a forest life, his native gifts, his culture, and his entire development would secure him a home only in the midst of civilization and refinement. In furtherance of this choice, it so happened that a ship lay in the harbor; one of those questionable cruisers, frequent at that day, which, without being absolutely outside the law, yet roamed over the sea with a remarkable irresponsibility of character. This vessel had recently arrived from the Spanish Main,[1] and, within three days' time, would sail for Bristol. Hester Prynne—whose vocation, as a self-enlisted Sister of Charity, had made her acquainted with the captain and his crew—could take upon herself to secure passage for two individuals and a child, with that secrecy which circumstances rendered desirable.

The minister had asked Hester, with no little interest, the precise time at which the vessel might leave. It would probably be on the fourth day from the present. "That is most fortunate!" he had said to himself. Now, why he considered it so very fortunate, we hesitate to reveal. Nevertheless,—to hold nothing back from the reader,—it was because, on the third day from the present, he was to preach the Election Sermon; and as such an occasion formed an honorable moment in the life of a New England clergyman, he could not have chanced upon a more suitable manner and time of ending his professional career. "At least, they shall say of me," thought this outstanding man, "that I leave no public duty unperformed, nor ill performed!" Sad, indeed, that a self-examination so profound and acute as this poor minister's should be so miserably deceived! We have had, and may still have, worse things to tell of him; but none, we apprehend, so pitiably weak; no evidence, at once so slight and undeniable of a disease, that had long since begun to eat into his

---

[1] Spanish Main: the Caribbean Sea

character. No man can wear one face to himself, and another to the multitude, without finally getting puzzled as to which is the true one.

The excitement of his feelings, as he returned from his interview with Hester, lent him unaccustomed physical energy, and hurried him townward at a rapid pace. The pathway among the woods seemed wilder, more uncouth with its rude natural obstacles, and less trodden by the foot of man, than he remembered it on his outward journey. But he leaped across the plashy[2] places, thrust himself through the clinging underbrush, climbed the ascent, plunged into the hollow, and overcame, in short, all the difficulties of the track, with an unweariable activity that astonished him. He recalled how feebly, and with what frequent pauses for breath, he had toiled over the same ground, only two days before. As he drew near the town, he took an impression of change from the series of familiar objects that presented themselves. It seemed not yesterday, not one, nor two, but many days, or even years ago, since he had quitted them. There, indeed, was each former trace of the street, as he remembered it, and all the peculiarities of the houses. Not the less, however, came this sense of change. The same was true regarding the acquaintances whom he met, and all the well-known shapes of human life, about the town. They looked neither older nor younger now; the beards of the aged were no whiter, nor could the creeping babe of yesterday walk on his feet to-day; it was impossible to describe in what respect they differed from the individuals on whom he had so recently bestowed a parting glance; and yet the minister's deepest sense told him there was a change. A similar impression struck him as he passed under the walls of his own church. The building had so very strange, and yet so familiar, an aspect, that Dimmesdale's mind vibrated between two ideas; either

[2] plashy: wet; marshy

that he had seen it only in a dream hitherto, or that he was dreaming about it now.

This phenomenon,[3] in the various shapes which it assumed, indicated no external change, but such a sudden and important change in the spectator of the familiar scene, that the intervening space of a single day had operated on his consciousness like the lapse of years. The minister's own will, and Hester's will, and the fate that grew between them, had wrought this transformation. It was the same town as heretofore; but it was not the same minister who returned from the forest. He might have said to the friends who greeted him,—"I am not the man for whom you take me! I left him yonder in the forest, withdrawn into a secret dell, by a mossy tree-trunk, and near a melancholy brook! Go seek your minister, and see if his emaciated figure, his thin cheek, his white, heavy, pain-wrinkled brow, be not flung down there, like a cast-off garment!"

Before he reached home, his inner man gave him other evidences of a revolution in the sphere of thought and feeling. At every step he was incited to do some strange, wild, wicked thing, with a sense that it would be at once involuntary and intentional; in spite of himself, yet growing out of a deeper self than that which opposed the impulse. For instance, he met one of his own deacons. The good old man addressed him with the paternal affection and patriarchal[4] privilege, which his venerable age, his upright and holy character, and his station in the Church, entitled him to use; and, joined with this, the deep, almost worshipping respect, which the minister's professional and private claims alike demanded. Now, during a conversation of some two or three moments between the Reverend Mr. Dimmesdale and this excellent and hoary-bearded deacon,

[3] phenomenon: observable condition
[4] patriarchal: worthy of reverence

it was only by the most careful self-control that the former could refrain from uttering certain blasphemous suggestions that rose into his mind, respecting the communion supper.

Again, another incident of the same nature. Hurrying along the street, he encountered the eldest female member of his church; a most pious old dame; poor, widowed, lonely, and with a heart as full of reminiscences about her dead husband and children, and her dead friends of long ago, as a burial ground is full of storied gravestones. Yet all this, which would else have been such heavy sorrow, was made almost a solemn joy to her devout old soul, by religious consolation and the truths of Scripture, with which she had fed herself for more than thirty years. And, since Dimmesdale had taken her in charge, the good old woman's chief earthly comfort was to meet her pastor, whether casually, or of set purpose, and be refreshed with a word of warm, fragrant, heaven-breathing Gospel truth, from his beloved lips. But, on this occasion, up to the moment of putting his lips to the old woman's ear, he could recall no text of Scripture, nor aught else, except a brief and, as it then appeared to him, unanswerable argument against the immortality of the soul. The instilment[5] thereof into her mind would probably have caused this aged sister to drop down dead at once, as by the effect of a strong poison. What he really did whisper, the minister could never afterwards recollect. There was, perhaps, a fortunate disorder in his utterance, which failed to impart any distinct idea to the good widow's comprehension. Assuredly, as the minister looked back, he beheld an expression of divine gratitude and ecstasy on her face.

Again a third instance. After parting from the old church-member, he met the youngest sister of them all. It was a maiden newly won—and won by his own sermon,

---

[5] instilment: implanting

on the Sabbath after his vigil. She was fair and pure as a lily that had bloomed in Paradise. The minister knew well that he was enshrined within the stainless sanctity of her heart, which hung its snowy curtains about his image, imparting to religion the warmth of love, and to love a religious purity. Satan, that afternoon, had surely led the poor young girl away from her mother's side, and thrown her into the pathway of this sorely tempted, or—shall we not rather say?—this lost and desperate man. As she drew near, the arch-fiend whispered to him to condense into small compass and drop into her tender bosom a germ of evil that would be sure to blossom darkly soon, and to bear black fruit. Such was his sense of power over this virgin soul, trusting him as she did, that the minister felt potent to blight all the field of innocence with but one wicked look, and develop all its opposite with but a word. So he held his Geneva cloak before his face, and hurried onward, making no sign of recognition, leaving the young sister to digest his rudeness as she might. She ransacked[6] her con-science,—which was full of harmless little matters, like her pocket or her work-bag,—and took herself to task, poor thing! for a thousand imaginary faults; and went about her household duties with swollen eyelids the next morning.

"What is it that haunts and tempts me thus?" cried the minister to himself, pausing in the street, and striking his forehead. "Am I mad? Am I given over utterly to the fiend? did I make a contract with him the forest, and sign it with my blood? And does he now summon me to its fulfilment, by suggesting the performance of every wicked-ness which his foul imagination can conceive?"

At the moment when the Reverend Mr. Dimmesdale thus communed with himself, old Mistress Hibbins, the reputed witch-lady, is said to have been passing by. She made a grand appearance; having on a high head-dress, a

---

[6] ransacked: searched thoroughly

rich gown of velvet, and a ruff done up with the famous yellow starch, of which Ann Turner,[7] her special friend, had taught her the secret, before this last good lady had been hanged for Sir Thomas Overbury's murder. Whether the witch had read the minister's thoughts or no, she stopped, looked shrewdly into his face, smiled craftily, and—though little given to converse with clergymen—began a conversation.

"So, Reverend Sir, you have made a visit into the forest, she observed, nodding her high head-dress at him. "The next time, I pray you to allow me only a fair warning, and I shall be proud to bear you company. Without taking overmuch upon myself, my good word will go far towards gaining any strange gentleman a fair reception from yonder sovereign you know of!"

"I profess, madam," answered the clergyman, with a grave bow such as her rank demanded, and his own good-breeding made imperative,—"I profess, on my conscience and character, that I am utterly bewildered as touching the purport[8] of your words! I went not into the forest to seek a sovereign; neither do I, at any future time, plan a visit thither, with a view to gaining the favor of such a personage. My one object was to greet that pious friend of mine, the Apostle Eliot, and to rejoice with him over the many precious souls he hath won from heathendom!"

"Ha, ha, ha!" cackled the old witch-lady, still nodding her high head-dress at him. "Well, well, we must needs talk thus in the daytime! You carry it off like an old hand! But at midnight, and in the forest, we shall have other talk together!"

She passed on with her aged stateliness, but often turning back her head and smiling at him, like one willing to recognize a secret intimacy of connection.

[7] Ann Turner: English murderess

[8] purport: meaning

"Have I then sold myself," thought the minister, "to the fiend whom, if men say true, this yellow-starched and velveted old hag has chosen for her prince and master!" Wretched minister! He had made a bargain very like it. Tempted by a dream of happiness, he had yielded himself, with deliberate choice, as he had never done before, to what he knew was deadly sin. And the infectious poison of that sin had been thus rapidly spread throughout his moral system. It had dulled all good impulses, and awakened all bad ones. Scorn, bitterness, unprovoked malignity and desire of ill, ridicule of whatever was good and holy,— all awoke, to tempt, even while they frightened him. And his encounter with old Mistress Hibbins, if it were a real incident, did but show his sympathy and fellowship with wicked mortals and the world of perverted spirits.

He had, by this time, reached his dwelling, on the edge of the burial-ground, and, hastening up the stairs, took refuge in his study. He was glad to have reached this shelter, without first betraying himself to the world by any of those strange and wicked eccentricities[9] to which he had been continually impelled while passing through the streets. He entered the accustomed room, and looked around him on its books, its windows, its fireplace, and the tapestried comfort of the walls, with the same feeling of strangeness that had haunted him throughout his walk from the forest-dell into and from the town. *Here* he had studied and written; *here,* gone through fast and vigil, and come forth half alive; *here* striven to pray; *here,* borne a hundred thousand agonies! There was the Bible, in its rich old Hebrew, with Moses and the Prophets speaking to him, and God's voice through all! There, on the table, with the inky pen beside it, was an unfinished sermon, with a sentence broken in the midst, where his thoughts had ceased to gush out upon the page, two days before. He knew that

[9] eccentricities: odd and unpredictable acts

it was himself, the thin and white-cheeked minister, who had done these things, and written thus far into the Election Sermon! But he seemed to stand apart, and eye this former self with scornful, pitying, but half-envious curiosity. *That* self was gone. Another man had returned out of the forest; a wiser one; with a knowledge of hidden mysteries which the simplicity of the former never could have reached. A bitter kind of knowledge that!

While occupied with these reflections, a knock came at the door, and the minister said, "Come in!"—not wholly devoid of an idea that he might behold an evil spirit. And so he did! It was old Roger Chillingworth. The minister stood, white and speechless, one hand on the Hebrew Scriptures, the other spread upon his breast.

"Welcome home, Reverend Sir," said the physician. "How found you that godly man, the Apostle Eliot? But, methinks, dear Sir, you look pale; as if the travel through the wilderness had been too sore for you. Will not my aid be requisite to put you in heart and strength to preach your Election Sermon?"

"Nay, I think not so," rejoined the clergyman. "My journey, the sight of the holy Apostle yonder, and the free air which I have breathed,—all these have done me good, after so long confinement in my study. I need no more of your drugs, my kind physician, good though they be, and administered by a friendly hand."

All this time, Roger Chillingworth was looking at the minister with the grave and intent regard of a physician towards his patient. But, in spite of this outward show, the latter was almost convinced of the old man's knowledge, or, at least, his suspicion, with respect to his own interview with Hester Prynne. The physician knew then, that, in the minister's regard, he was no longer a trusted friend, but his bitterest enemy. So much being known, it would appear natural that a part of it should be expressed. It is singular, however, how long a time often passes before words embody things; and with what security two persons, who choose to avoid a certain subject, may approach its very edge, and retire without disturbing it. Thus, the minister felt no fear that Roger Chillingworth would touch, in express words, upon the real position which they sustained towards one another. Yet did the physician, in his dark way, creep frightfully near the secret.

"Were it not better," said he, "that you use my poor skill tonight? Really, dear Sir, we must take pains to make you strong and vigorous for this occasion of the Election discourse. The people look for great things from you; fearing that another year may come about, and find their pastor gone."

"Yea, to another world," replied the minister, with pious resignation. "Heaven grant it be a better one; for, in good sooth, I hardly think to tarry with my flock through another year! But, as for your medicine, kind Sir, in my present frame of body, I need it not."

"I joy to hear it," answered the physician. "It may be that my remedies, so long administered in vain, now begin to take due effect. Happy man were I, and well deserving New England's gratitude, could I achieve this cure!"

"I thank you from my heart, most watchful friend," said Dimmesdale, with a solemn smile. "I thank you, and can but reward your good deeds with my prayers."

"A good man's prayers are gold!" rejoined old Roger Chillingworth, as he left. "Yea, they are the current gold coin of the New Jerusalem, with the King's own mint-mark on them!"

Left alone, the minister summoned a servant and requested food, which he ate greedily. Then, flinging the already written pages of the Election Sermon into the fire, he forthwith began another, writing with such impulsive flow of thought and emotion, that he fancied himself inspired; and only wondered that Heaven saw fit to transmit the grand and solemn music of its oracles through so foul an organ-pipe as he. However, leaving that mystery to solve itself, or to go unsolved forever, he drove his task onward, with haste and ecstasy. Thus the night fled away, as if it were a winged steed, and he careering on it; morning came, and at last sunrise threw a golden beam into the study and laid it right across the minister's bedazzled eyes. There he was, with pen still between his fingers, and a vast, immeasurable tract of written space behind him!

21   *The New England Holiday*

Early in the morning of the day on which the new Governor was to receive his office at the hands of the people, Hester Prynne and little Pearl came into the market place. It was already thronged with the skilled laborers and mechanics[1] and other common inhabitants of the town, in considerable numbers; among whom, likewise, were many rough figures, whose dress of deer-skins marked them as belonging to some of the forest settlements, which surrounded the little metropolis of the colony.

On this public holiday, as on all other occasions, for seven years past, Hester was clad in a garment of coarse gray cloth. Not more by its hue than by some indescribable peculiarity in its fashion, it had the effect of making her fade personally out of sight and outline; while, again, the scarlet letter brought her back from this twilight indistinctness, and revealed her under the moral aspect of its own illumination. Her face, so long familiar to the townspeople, showed the marble quietude which they were accustomed to behold there.

Pearl as decked out with airy gayety. It would have been impossible to guess that this bright and sunny apparition owed its existence to the shape of gloomy gray; or

[1] mechanics: old word for manual laborers

that a fancy, at once so gorgeous and so delicate as must have been requisite to contrive the child's apparel, was the same that had achieved a task perhaps more difficult, in imparting so distinct a peculiarity to Hester's simple robe. The dress, so proper was it to little Pearl, seemed an effluence,[2] or inevitable development and outward manifestation of her character, no more to be separated from her than the many-hued brilliancy from a butterfly's wing, or the painted glory from the leaf of a bright flower. As with these, so with the child; her garb was all one with her nature. On this eventful day, moreover, there was a certain singular uneasiness and excitement in her mood, resembling nothing so much as the shimmer of a diamond, that sparkles and flashes with the varied throbbings of the breast on which it is displayed.

This emotion made her flit with a bird-like movement, rather than walk by her mother's side. She broke into

[2] effluence: something flowing forth

shouts of wild, inarticulate, and piercing music. When they reached the market place, she became still more restless, on perceiving the stir and bustle that enlivened the spot; for it was usually more like the broad and lonesome green before a village meeting house, than the centre of a town's business.

"Why, what is this, mother?" cried she. "Why have all the people left their work to-day? Is it a play-day for the whole world? See, there is the blacksmith! He has washed his sooty face, and put on his Sabbath-day clothes, and looks as if he would gladly be merry, if any kind body would only teach him how! And there is Master Brackett, the old jailer, nodding and smiling at me. Why does he do so, mother?"

"He remembers you as a little babe, my child," answered Hester.

"He should not nod and smile at me, for all that,—the black, grim, ugly-eyed old man!" said Pearl. "He may nod at thee, if he will; for thou art clad in gray, and wearest the scarlet letter. But see, mother, how many strange people, and Indians among them, and sailors! What have they all come to do, here in the market place?"

"They wait to see the procession pass," said Hester. "For the Governor and the magistrates are to go by, and the ministers, and all the great and good people, with the music and the soldiers marching before them."

"And will the minister be there?" asked Pearl. "And will he hold out both his hands to me, as when thou ledst me to him from the brook-side?"

"He will be there, child," answered her mother. "But he will not greet you to-day; nor must you greet him."

"What a strange, sad man is he!" said the child, as if speaking partly to herself. "In the dark night-time he calls us to him, and holds thy hand and mine, as when we stood with him on the scaffold yonder. And in the deep forest, where only the old trees can hear, and the strip of sky see it, he talks with thee, sitting on a heap of moss! And he kisses my forehead, too, so that the little brook would hardly wash it off! But here, in the sunny day, and among all the people, he knows us not; nor must we know him! A strange, sad man is he, with his hand always over his heart!"

"Be quiet, Pearl! You do not understand these things," said her mother. "Think not now of the minister, but look about you, and see how cheery is everybody to-day. The children have come from school, and the grown people from their workshops and their fields, on purpose to be happy. For, to-day, a new man is beginning to rule over them; and so they make merry and rejoice; as if a good and golden year were at length to pass over the poor old world!"

It was Hester said, in regard to the unusual jollity that brightened the faces of the people. Into this holiday season of the year—as it already was, and continued to be during the greater part of two centuries—the Puritans compressed whatever mirth and public joy they considered allowable to human weakness; thereby so far dispelling the customary cloud, that, for the space of a single holiday, they appeared scarcely more grave than most other communities at a period of general affliction.

But perhaps we exaggerate the gray or sable tinge, which undoubtedly characterized the mood and manners of the age. The persons now in the market place of Boston had not been born to an inheritance of Puritanic gloom. They were native Englishmen, whose fathers had lived in the sunny richness of the Elizabethan epoch; a time when the life of England, viewed as one great mass, would appear to have been as stately, magnificent, and joyous, as the world has ever witnessed. Had they followed their hereditary taste, the New England settlers would have illustrated all events of public importance by bonfires, banquets, pageantries and processions. Nor would it have been impracticable, in the observance of majestic ceremonies, to combine mirthful recreation with solemnity, and to give, as it were, a grotesque and brilliant embroidery to the great robe of state, which a nation, at such festivals, puts on. There was some shadow of an attempt of this kind in the mode of celebrating the day on which the political year of the colony commenced. The dim reflection of a remembered splendor, a colorless repetition of what they had beheld in proud old London,—we will not say at a royal coronation, but at a Lord Mayor's show,—might be traced in the customs which our forefathers instituted, with reference to the annual installation of magistrates. The fathers and founders of the commonwealth—the statesman, the priest, and the soldier-deemed it a duty then to assume the outward state and majesty, which was looked upon as the proper garb of public or social eminence. All came forth, to move in procession before the people's eye, and thus impart a needed dignity to the simple framework of a government so newly constructed.

Then, too, the people were encouraged, in relaxing the severe and close application to their various modes of rugged industry, which, at all other times, seemed of the same piece and material with their religion. Here, it is true, were none of the appliances which popular merriment would so readily have found in the England of Elizabeth's time,[3] or that of James;[4] no rude shows of the theatrical kind; no minstrel, with his harp and legendary ballad, no wandering singer with an ape dancing to his music; no juggler, with his tricks of mimic witchcraft; no Merry Andrew,[5] to stir up the multitude with stale jests. All such masters of the several branches of fun and frolic would have been sternly repressed, not only by the rigid discipline of law, but by the general sentiment which gives law its vitality. Not the less, however, the great, honest face of the people smiled grimly, perhaps, but widely too. Nor were sports wanting, such as the colonists had witnessed, and shared in, long ago, at the country fairs and on the village-greens of England; and which it was thought well to keep alive on this new soil, for the sake of the courage and manliness that were essential in them. Wrestling-matches were seen here and there about the market place; in one corner there was a friendly bout at quarter-staff; and— what attracted most interest of all—on the platform of the pillory, already so noted in our pages, two masters of defence were commencing an exhibition with the shield and broadsword.

It may not be too much to affirm, on the whole (the people being then in the first stages of joyless deportment,

[3] Elizabeth's time: Queen Elizabeth, (1533–1603)

[4] James: James I of England, (1566–1625)

[5] Merry Andrew: a clown

and the offspring of sires who had known how to be merry, in their day), that they would compare favorably, in point of holiday keeping, with their descendants, even at so long an interval as ourselves. Their immediate posterity, the generation next to the early emigrants, wore the blackest shade of Puritanism, and so darkened the national visage with it, that all the subsequent years have not sufficed to clear it up.

The picture of human life in the market place, though its general tint was the sad gray, brown, or black of the English emigrants, was yet enlivened by some diversity of hue. A party of Indians—in their savage finery of curiously embroidered deer-skin robes, wampum-belts, red and yellow paint, and feathers, and armed with bow and arrow and stone-headed spear—stood apart, with countenances of unbending gravity, beyond what even the Puritan aspect could attain. Nor, wild as were these painted barbarians, were they the wildest feature of the scene. This distinction could more justly be claimed by some mariners,—a part of the crew of the vessel from the Spanish Main,—who had come ashore to see the doings on Election Day. They were rough-looking desperadoes, with sun-blackened faces, and long beards; their wide, short trousers were confined about the waist by belts, often clasped with a rough plate of gold, and sustaining always a long knife, and, in some instances, a sword. From beneath their broad-rimmed hats gleamed eyes which, even in good-nature and merriment, had a kind of animal fierceness. They violated, without fear or scruple, the rules of behavior that were binding on all others, smoking tobacco under the beadle's very nose, although each whiff would have cost a townsman a shilling; and quaffing, at their pleasure, drafts of wine or brandy from pocket-flasks, which they freely tendered to the gaping crowd. It remarkably characterized the incomplete morality of the age, rigid as we call it, that a license was allowed the seafaring class, not merely for their freaks[6] on shore, but for far more desperate deeds at sea. The sailor *of that day* would go near to be arraigned as a pirate in *our own*. There could be little doubt, for instance, that this very ship's crew, though no unfavorable specimens of the nautical brotherhood, had been guilty of plundering attacks on Spanish commerce, such as would have imperilled all their necks in a modern court of justice.

But the sea, in those old times, heaved, swelled, and foamed, very much at its own will, or subject only to the tempestuous wind, with hardly any attempt at regulation by human law. The pirate on the wave might relinquish his calling, and become at once, if he chose, a man of honesty and piety on land; nor, even in the full career of his reckless life, was he regarded as a personage with whom it was disreputable to traffic, or casually associate. Thus, the Puritan elders, in their black cloaks, starched bands, and steeple-crowned hats, smiled at the clamor and rude deportment of these jolly seafaring men; and it excited no surprise when so respectable a citizen as old Roger Chillingworth, the physician, was seen to enter the market place, talking with the commander of the questionable vessel.

The latter was by far the most showy and gallant figure, so far as apparel went, to be seen among the multitude. He wore a profusion of ribbons on his garment, and gold-lace on his hat, which was also encircled by a gold chain, and surmounted with a feather. There was a sword at his side, and a sword-cut on his forehead, which, by the arrangement of his hair, he seemed anxious rather to display than hide. A landsman could hardly have worn this garb and shown his face, and worn and shown them both with such a brave air, without undergoing questioning before a magistrate, and probably incurring fine or imprisonment, or perhaps an exhibition in the stocks.

---

[6] freaks: unusual or abnormal behavior

After parting from the physician, the commander of the Bristol ship strolled idly through the market place; until happening to approach the spot where Hester Prynne was standing, he appeared to recognize, and did not hesitate to address her. As was usually the case wherever Hester stood, a small vacant area—a sort of magic circle—had formed itself about her, into which, though the people were elbowing one another at a little distance, none ventured, or felt disposed, to intrude. It was a forcible type of the moral loneliness in which the scarlet letter enveloped its fated wearer; partly by her own reserve, and partly by the instinctive, though no longer so unkindly, withdrawal of her fellow-creatures. Now, if never before, it answered a good purpose, by enabling Hester and the seaman to speak together without being overheard; and so changed was Hester Prynne's repute before the public, that the matron in town most eminent for rigid morality could not have held such conversation with less scandal than herself.

"So, mistress," said the mariner, "I must bid the steward make ready one more berth than you bargained for! No fear of ship-fever this voyage! What with the ship's surgeon and this other doctor, our only danger will be from drug or pill; more by token, as there is a lot of druggist's stuff aboard, which I traded for with a Spanish vessel."

"What mean you?" inquired Hester, more startled than she permitted to appear. "Have you *another* passenger?"

"Why, know you not," cried the shipmaster, "that this physician here—Chillingworth, he calls himself—is minded to try my cabin-fare with you? Ay, ay, you must have known it; for he tells me he is of your party, and a close friend to the gentleman you spoke of,—he that is in peril from these sour old Puritan rulers!"

"They know each other well, indeed," replied Hester, with an air of calmness, though in the utmost fear. "They have long dwelt together."

Nothing further passed between the mariner and Hester Prynne. But, at that instant, she beheld old Roger Chillingworth himself, standing in the remotest corner of the market place, and smiling at her; a smile which—across the wide and bustling square, and through all the talk and laughter, and various thoughts, moods, and interests of the crowd—conveyed secret and fearful meaning.

22 *The Procession*

Before Hester Prynne could collect her thoughts, and consider what was to be done in this new and startling aspect of affairs, the sound of military music was heard approaching along a nearby street. It denoted the advance of the procession of magistrates and citizens, on its way to the meeting house; where, in compliance with a custom thus early established, and ever since observed, the Reverend Mr. Dimmesdale was to deliver an Election Sermon.

Soon the head of the procession showed itself, with a slow and stately march, turning a corner and making its way across the market place. First came the music. It comprised a variety of instruments, perhaps imperfectly suited to one another, and played with no great skill. Little Pearl at first clapped her hands, but then lost, for an instant, the restless agitation that had kept her in a continual state of emotion throughout the morning; she gazed silently and seemed to be borne upward, like a floating seabird, on the long heaves and swells of sound. But she was brought back to her former mood by the shimmer of the sunshine on the weapons and bright armor of the military company, which followed after the music, and formed the honorary escort of the procession.

Next in order to the magistrates came the young and distinguished divine, from whose lips the discourse of the

anniversary was expected. His was the profession, at that era, in which intellectual ability showed itself far more than in political life; for—leaving a higher motive out of the question—it offered inducements powerful enough, in the almost worshipping respect of the community, to win the most aspiring ambition into its service. Even political power—as in the case of Increase Mather[1]—was within the grasp of a successful priest.

It was the observation of those who beheld the minister now that never since he first set his foot on the New England shore, had he exhibited such energy as was seen in the gait and air with which he kept his pace in the procession. There was no feebleness of step, as at other times; his frame was not bent; nor did his hand rest upon his heart. Yet, if the clergyman were rightly viewed, his strength seemed not physical, but spiritual. It might be the exhilaration of that potent cordial[2] which is distilled only in the furnace glow of earnest and long-continued thought. Or, perhaps, his sensitive temperament was strengthened by the loud and piercing music, that swelled heavenward, and uplifted him on its ascending wave. Nevertheless, so abstracted was his look, that it might be questioned whether he even heard the music. There was his body, moving onward, and with an unaccustomed force. But where as his *mind?* Far and deep in its own region, busying itself, with preternatural activity, to marshal a procession of stately thoughts that were soon to issue thence: and so he saw nothing, heard nothing, knew nothing, of what was around him; but the spiritual element took up the feeble frame, and carried it along, unconscious of the burden, and converting it to spirit like itself.

Hester Prynne, gazing steadfastly at the clergyman,

[1] Increase Mather: noted churchman and president of Harvard (1639–1723)

[2] cordial: a medicine or drink that stimulates the heart

felt a dreary influence come over her, but wherefore or
whence she knew not; unless that he seemed so remote
from her own sphere, and utterly beyond her reach. One
glance of recognition, she had imagined, must needs pass
between them. She thought of the dim forest, with its little
dell of solitude, and love, and anguish, and the mossy tree-
trunk, where, sitting hand in hand, they had mingled their
sad and passionate talk with the melancholy murmur of
the brook. How deeply had they known each other then!
And was this the man? She hardly knew him now! Her
spirit sank with the idea that all must have been a delusion,
and that, vividly as she had dreamed it, there could be no
real bond between the clergyman and herself. And thus
much of woman was there in Hester, that she could
scarcely forgive him,—least of all now, when the heavy
footstep of their approaching Fate might be heard, nearer,
nearer, nearer!—for being able so completely to withdraw
himself from their mutual world; while she groped darkly,
and stretched forth her cold hands, and found him not.

Pearl either saw and responded to her mother's feelings, or herself felt the remoteness and intangibility that
had fallen around the minister. While the procession
passed, the child was uneasy, fluttering up and down, like
a bird on the point of taking flight. When it had gone by,
she looked up into Hester's face.

"Mother," said she, "was that the same minister who
kissed me by the brook?"

"Hold thy peace, Pearl!" whispered her mother. "We
must not always talk in the market place of what happens
to us in the forest."

"I could not be sure that it was he; so strange he
looked," continued the child. "Else I would have run to
him, and bid him kiss me now, before all the people; even
as he did yonder among the dark old trees. What would
the minister have said, mother? Would he have clapped

his hand over his heart, and scowled at me, and bid me be gone?"

"What should he say, Pearl," answered Hester, "save that it was no time to kiss, and that kisses are not to be given in the market place? Well for you, foolish child, that you did not speak to him!"

Another shade of the same sentiment, in reference to Mr. Dimmesdale, was expressed by a person whose eccentricities led her to do what few of the townspeople would have ventured on: to begin a public conversation with the wearer of the scarlet letter. It was Mistress Hibbins, who, arrayed in great magnificence, with a triple ruff, an embroidered stomacher,[3] a gown of rich velvet, and gold-headed cane, had come forth to see the procession. As this ancient lady had the renown (which subsequently cost her her life) of being a principal actor in all the works of black magic that were continually going forward, the crowd gave way before her, seeming to fear the touch of her garment, as if it carried the plague among its gorgeous folds. Seen with Hester Prynne,—kindly as so many *now* felt towards the latter,—the dread inspired by Mistress Hibbins was doubled, and caused a general movement from that part of the market place in which the two women stood.

"Now, what mortal imagination could conceive it!" whispered the old lady, confidently, to Hester. "Yonder divine man! That saint on earth, as the people deem him, and as—I must needs say—he really looks! Who, now, that saw him pass in the procession, would think how little while it is since he went forth out of his study to take an airing in the forest! Aha! we know what that means, Hester Prynne! But, truly, forsooth, I find it hard to believe him the same man. But this minister! Couldst thou surely tell, Hester, whether he was the same man that encountered thee on the forest-path?"

[3] stomacher: an ornamental garment worn by men and women

"Madam, I know not of what you speak," answered Hester Prynne, feeling Mistress Hibbins to be of infirm mind. "It is not for me to talk lightly of a learned and pious minister of the Word, like the Reverend Mr. Dimmesdale!"

"Fie, woman, fie!" cried the old lady, shaking her finger at Hester. "Dost thou think I have been to the forest so many times, and have yet no skill to know who else has been there? Yea; though no leaf of the wild garlands, which they wore while they danced be left in their hair! I know thee, Hester; for I behold the token. We may all see it in the sunshine; and it glows like a red flame in the dark. Thou wearest it openly; so there need be no question about that. But this minister! Let me tell thee, in thine ear! When the Black Man sees one of his own servants, signed and sealed, so shy of owning to the bond as is the Reverend Mr. Dimmesdale, he hath a way of ordering matters so that the mark shall be disclosed in open daylight to the eyes of all the world! What is it that the minister seeks to hide, with his hand always over his heart? Ha, Hester Prynne!"

"What is it, good Mistress Hibbins?" eagerly asked little Pearl. "Hast thou seen it?"

"No matter, darling!" responded Mistress Hibbins, making Pearl a profound bow. "Thou thyself wilt see it, one time or another. They say, child, thou art of the lineage of the Prince of the Air![4] Wilt thou ride with me, some fine night, to see thy father? Then thou shalt know why the minister keeps his hand over his heart!"

Laughing so shrilly that all the market place could hear her, the weird old lady took her departure.

By this time the preliminary prayer had been offered in the meeting house, and the accents of the minister were heard commencing his discourse. An irresistible feeling kept Hester near the spot. As the sacred edifice was too much thronged to admit another auditor, she took up her

[4] Prince of the Air: one of the many names for Satan

position close beside the scaffold of the pillory. It was sufficiently close to bring the whole sermon to her ears, in the shape of an indistinct but varied murmur and flow of the minister's peculiar voice.

This vocal organ was in itself a rich endowment; insomuch that a listener, comprehending nothing of the language in which the preacher spoke, might still have been swayed to and fro by the mere tone. Like all other music, it breathed passion and pathos, and emotions high or tender, in a tongue native to the human heart, wherever educated. Muffled as the sound was by its passage through the church-walls, Hester Prynne listened so intently, and sympathized so intimately, that the sermon had a meaning for her, entirely apart from its indistinguishable words. These, perhaps, if more distinctly heard, might have been only a grosser medium, and have clogged the spiritual sense. Now she caught the low undertone, as of the wind sinking down to repose itself; then ascended with it, as it rose through progressive gradations of sweetness and power, until its volume seemed to envelop her with an atmosphere of awe and solemn grandeur. And yet, majestic as the voice sometimes became, there was forever in it an essential character of plaintiveness.[5]

During all this time, Hester stood, statue-like, at the foot of the scaffold. If the minister's voice had not kept her there, there would nevertheless have been an inevitable magnetism in that spot, whence she dated the first hour of her life of ignominy. There was a sense within her that her whole orb of life, both before and after, was connected with this spot, as with the one point that gave it unity.

Little Pearl, meanwhile, had quitted her mother's side, and was playing about the market place. She made the sombre crowd cheerful by her erratic and glistening ray. She had an undulating, but, oftentimes, a sharp, irregular

[5] plaintiveness: sorrowfulness

movement. It indicated the restless vivacity of her spirit, which to-day was doubly indefatigable in its tiptoe dance, because it was played upon and vibrated with her mother's disquietude. Whenever Pearl saw anything to excite her ever-active and wandering curiosity, she flew thitherward, and seized upon that man or thing as her own property, so far as she desired it; but without yielding the minutest degree of control over her motions in requital. The Puritans looked on, and, if they smiled, were none the less inclined to pronounce the child a demon offspring, from the indescribable charm of beauty and eccentricity that shone through her little figure, and sparkled with its activity. She ran and looked the wild Indian in the face, until he grew conscious of a nature wilder than his own. Thence, with native audacity, but still with a reserve as characteristic, she flew into the midst of a group of mariners, the swarthy-cheeked wild men of the ocean, as the Indians are of the land; and they gazed wonderingly and admiringly at Pearl, as if a flake of sea-foam had taken the shape of a little maid.

One of these seafaring men—the shipmaster, indeed, who had spoken to Hester Prynne—was so smitten with Pearl, that he attempted to catch her, with purpose to snatch a kiss. Finding it as impossible to touch her as to catch a humming-bird in the air, he took from his hat the gold chain that was twisted about it, and threw it to the child. Pearl immediately twined it around her neck and waist with such happy skill, that, once seen there, it became a part of her, and difficult to imagine her without it.

"Thy mother is yonder woman with the scarlet letter," said the seaman. "Wilt thou carry her a message from me?"

"If the message pleases me, I will," answered Pearl.

"Then tell her," rejoined he, "that I spake again with the hump-shouldered old doctor, and he engages to bring his friend, the gentleman she knows, aboard with him. So let thy mother take no thought, save for herself and thee. Wilt thou tell her this, thou witch-baby?"

"Mistress Hibbins says my father is the Prince of the Air!" cried Pearl, with a naughty smile. "If thou callest me that ill name, I shall tell him of thee, and he will chase thy ship with a tempest!"

Pursuing a zigzag course across the market place, the child returned to her mother, and communicated what the mariner had said. Hester's strong, calm, steadfastly enduring spirit almost sank, at last, on beholding this dark and grim countenance of an inevitable doom, which—at the moment when a passage seemed to open for the minister and herself out of their maze of misery—showed itself, with an unrelenting smile, right in the midst of their path.

With her mind harassed by the terrible perplexity in which the shipmaster's news involved her, she was also subjected to another trial. There were many people present, from the country round about, who had often *heard* of the scarlet letter, and to whom it had been made terrific by a hundred rumors, but who had never seen it. These, after exhausting other modes of amusement, now thronged about Hester Prynne with rude and boorish intrusiveness. Unscrupulous as it was, however, it could not bring them nearer than a distance of several yards. At that distance they accordingly stood, fixed by the centrifugal force of the repugnance which the mystic symbol inspired. The whole gang of sailors, likewise, observing the press of spectators, and learning the purport of the scarlet letter, came and thrust their sunburnt and rough-looking faces into the ring. Even the Indians were affected by the white man's curiosity, and, gliding through the crowd, fastened their snake-like black eyes on Hester's bosom; conceiving, perhaps, that the wearer of this brilliantly embroidered badge must needs be a personage[6] of high dignity among her

---

[6] personage: important person

own people. Lastly, the inhabitants of the town (their own interest in this worn-out subject languidly reviving itself, by sympathy with what they saw others feel) lounged idly to the same quarter, and tormented Hester Prynne, perhaps more than all the rest, by their cool, well-acquainted gaze at her familiar shame. Hester saw and recognized the self-same faces of that group of matrons, who had awaited her forthcoming from the prison-door, seven years ago; all save one, the youngest and most compassionate among them, whose burial robe she had since made. At the final hour, when she was so soon to fling aside the burning letter, it had strangely become the center of more remark and excitement, and was thus made to burn her breast more painfully than at any time since the first day she put it on.

While Hester stood in that "magic circle" of ignominy, where the cunning cruelty of her sentence seemed to have fixed her forever, the admirable preacher was looking down from the sacred pulpit upon an audience whose very inmost spirits had yielded to his control. The sainted minister in the church! The woman of the scarlet letter in the market place! What imagination would have dared to surmise that the same scorching brand of shame was on them *both!*

23 *The Revelation of the Scarlet Letter*

The eloquent voice, on which the souls of the listening audience had been borne aloft as on the swelling waves of the sea, at length came to a pause. There was a momentary silence, profound as what should follow the utterance of oracles.[1] Then ensued a murmur and half-hushed tumult; as if the listeners, released from the high spell that had transported them into the region of another's mind, were returning into themselves, with all their awe and wonder still heavy on them. In a moment more, the crowd began to gush forth from the doors of the church.

In the open air their rapture broke into speech. The street and the market place absolutely babbled, from side to side, with applause of the minister. His hearers could not rest until they had told one another of what each knew better than he could tell or hear. According to their united testimony, never had man spoken in so wise, so high, and so holy a spirit, as he that spake this day; never had inspiration breathed through mortal lips more evidently than it did through his. Its influence could be seen descending upon him, and possessing him, and continually lifting him out of the written words before him, and filling him with ideas that must have been as marvellous to himself as to

[1] oracles: persons believed to be in communication with a deity and able to foresee future events

his audience. The minister's subject had been the relation between the Deity and the communities of mankind, with special reference to the New England which they were here planting in the wilderness. But, throughout it all, and through the whole discourse, there had been a certain deep, sad undertone of pathos,[2] which could not be interpreted otherwise than as the natural regret of one so soon to pass away. Yes; their minister whom they so loved—and who so loved them all, that he could not depart heavenward without a sigh—had the foreboding of untimely death upon him, and would soon leave them! This idea of his short stay on earth gave the last emphasis to the effect which the preacher had produced; it was as if an angel, in his passage to the skies, had shaken his bright wings over the people for an instant and had shed down a shower of golden truths upon them.

Thus, there had come to the Reverend Arthur Dimmesdale—as to most men, in their various spheres, though seldom recognized until they see it far behind them—an epoch of life more brilliant and full of triumph than any previous one, or than any which could hereafter be. He stood, at this moment, on the very proudest eminence of superiority, to which the gifts of intellect, rich lore, eloquence, and a reputation of whitest sanctity, could exalt a clergyman in New England's earliest days, when the professional character was of itself a lofty pedestal. Such was the position which the minister occupied, as he bowed his head forward on the cushions of the pulpit, at the close of his Election Sermon. Meanwhile Hester Prynne was standing beside the scaffold of the pillory, with the scarlet letter still burning on her breast!

Now was heard again the clangor of music, and the measured tramp of the military escort, issuing from the church-door. The procession was to be marshalled thence

[2] pathos: a quality that arouses pity or sympathy

to the town-hall, where a solemn banquet would complete the ceremonies of the day.

Once more, therefore, the train of venerable[3] and majestic fathers was seen moving through a broad pathway of the people, who drew back reverently, on either side, as the Governor and the magistrates, the old and wise men, the holy ministers, and all that were eminent and renowned, advanced into the midst of them. When they were fairly in the market place, their presence was greeted by a shout. This was felt to be an irrepressible outburst of enthusiasm kindled in the auditors by that high strain of eloquence which was still reverberating in their ears. Each felt the impulse in himself, and caught it from his neighbor. Within the church, it had already been kept down; but now, beneath the sky, it pealed upward to the highest point of heaven. Never, from the soil of New England, had gone up such a shout! Never, on New England soil, had stood a man so honored by his mortal brethren as the preacher!

As the ranks of military men and civil fathers moved onward, all eyes were turned to the point where the minister was seen approaching them. The shout died into a murmur, as one portion of the crowd after another obtained a glimpse of him. How feeble and pale he looked, amid all his triumph! The energy, the inspiration which had held him up until he should have delivered the sacred message that brought its own strength along with it from Heaven was withdrawn, now that it had so faithfully performed its office. The glow, which they had just beheld burning on his cheek, was extinguished now, like a flame that sinks down among the decaying embers. It seemed hardly the face of a man alive, with such a deathlike hue; it was hardly a man with life in him that tottered on his path so nervelessly, yet tottered, and did not fall!

[3] venerable: worthy of respect because of age and dignity

One of his clerical brethren,—it was the venerable John Wilson,—observing the state in which he was left by the retiring wave of intellect and feeling, stepped forward hastily to offer his support. The minister tremulously, but decidedly, repelled the old man's arm. He still walked onward, if that movement could be so described, which rather resembled the wavering effort of an infant with its mother's arms outstretched to tempt him forward. And now, almost imperceptible as were the latter steps of his progress, he had come opposite the well-remembered and weather-darkened scaffold, where, long since, with all that dreary lapse of time between, Hester Prynne had encountered the world's ignominious stare. There she stood; holding little Pearl by the hand! And there was the scarlet letter on her breast! The minister here made a pause, although the music still played the stately and rejoicing march to which the procession moved. It summoned him onward,—onward to the festival!—but here he made a pause.

Bellingham, for the last few moments, had kept an anxious eye upon him. He now left his own place in the procession, and advanced to give assistance, judging, from Dimmesdale's aspect, that he must otherwise inevitably fall. But there was something in the latter's expression that warned back the magistrate, although ordinarily he was not a man to readily obey the vague intimations that pass from one spirit to another. This earthly faintness was, in their view, only another phase of the minister's spiritual strength; nor would it have seemed a miracle too high to be wrought for one so holy, had he ascended before their eyes, waxing dimmer and brighter, and fading at last into the light of heaven.

He turned towards the scaffold, and stretched forth his arms.

"Hester," said he, "come hither! Come, my little Pearl!"

It was a ghastly look with which he regarded them;

but there was something both tender and strangely triumphant in it. The child, with the bird-like motion which was
one of her characteristics, flew to him, and clasped her
arms about his knees. Hester Prynne—slowly, as if impelled by fate, and against her will—likewise drew near,
but paused before she reached him. At this instant, old
Roger Chillingworth thrust himself through the crowd, to
snatch back his victim from what he sought to do! The old
man rushed forward, and caught the minister by the arm.

"Madman, stop! what is your purpose?" whispered he.
"Wave back that woman! Cast off this child! All shall be
well! Do not blacken your fame, and die in dishonor! I can
yet save you! Would you bring infamy on your sacred
profession?"

"Ha, tempter! I think you are too late!" answered the
minister, encountering his eye, fearfully, but firmly. "Your

power is not what it was! With God's help I shall escape you now!"

He again extended his hand to the woman of the scarlet letter.

"Hester Prynne," cried he, with a piercing earnestness, "in the name of Him, so terrible and so merciful, who gives me grace, at this last moment, to do what—for my own heavy sin and miserable agony—I withheld myself from doing seven years ago, come hither now, and entwine thy strength about me! *Thy* strength, Hester; but let it be guided by the will which God hath granted me! This wretched and wronged old man is opposing it with all his might! with all his own might, and the fiend's! Come, Hester, come! Support me up yonder scaffold! Come!"

The crowd was in a tumult. Men of rank and dignity, who stood immediately around the clergyman, were so taken by surprise, and so perplexed as to the meaning of what they saw,—unable to accept the explanation which most readily presented itself, or to imagine any other,—that they remained silent spectators of the judgment which Providence seemed about to work. They beheld the minister, leaning on Hester's shoulder, and supported by her arm around him, approach the scaffold, and ascend its steps; while still the little hand of the little child was clasped in his. Old Roger Chillingworth followed, as one intimately connected with the drama of guilt and sorrow in which they had all been actors, and well entitled, therefore, to be present at its closing scene.

"Hadst thou sought the whole earth over," said he, looking darkly at the clergyman, "there was no one place so secret,—no high place nor lowly place, where thou couldst have escaped me,—save on this very scaffold!"

"Thanks be to Him who hath led me hither!" answered the minister.

Yet he trembled, and turned to Hester with doubt and anxiety in his eyes, not the less evidently betrayed because there was a feeble smile upon his lips.

"Is not this better," murmured he, "than what we dreamed of in the forest?"

"I know not! I know not!" she hurriedly replied. "Better? Yea; so we may both die, and little Pearl die with us!"

"For thee and Pearl, be it as God shall order," said the minister; "and God is merciful! Let me now do the will which He hath made plain before my sight. For, Hester, I am a dying man. So let me make haste to take my shame upon me!"

Partly supported by Hester Prynne, and holding one hand of little Pearl's, he turned to the dignified and venerable rulers; to the holy ministers, who were his brethren; to the people, whose great heart was thoroughly appalled, yet full of tearful sympathy, as knowing that some deep life-matter—which, if full of sin, was full of anguish and repentance likewise—was now to be laid open to them. The sun shone down upon the clergyman, and gave a sharpness to his figure, as he stood out from all the earth, to put in his plea of Guilty at the bar of Eternal Justice.

"People of New England!" cried he, with a voice that rose over them, high, solemn, and majestic, "ye, that have loved me!—ye, that have deemed me holy!—behold me here, the one sinner of the world! At last—at last!—I stand upon the spot where seven years since, I should have stood; here, with this woman, whose arm, more than the little strength wherewith I have crept hitherward, sustains me, at this dreadful moment, from grovelling down upon my face! Lo, the scarlet letter which Hester wears! Ye have all shuddered at it! Wherever her walk hath been,—whenever, so miserably burdened, she may have hoped to find repose,—it hath cast a lurid gleam of awe and horrible repugnance[4] round about her. But there stood one in the midst of you, at whose brand of sin and infamy ye have not shuddered!"

It seemed, at this point, as if the minister must leave the remainder of his secret undisclosed. But he fought back the bodily weakness, and the faintness of heart, that was striving for the mastery with him. He threw off all assistance, and stepped passionately forward a pace before the woman and the child.

"It was on him!" he continued, with a kind of fierceness,—so determined was he to speak out the whole. "God's eye beheld it! The angels were forever pointing at it. The Devil knew it well, and scratched it continually with his burning finger! But he hid it cunningly from men, and walked among you with the mien of a spirit, mournful, because so pure in a sinful world!—and sad, because he missed his heavenly kindred! Now, at the death-hour, he

[4] repugnance: extreme dislike

stands up before you. He bids you look again at Hester's scarlet letter! He tells you, that, with all its mysterious horror, it is but the shadow of what *he* bears on his own breast, and that even this, his own red stigma,[5] is no more than the type of what has seared his inmost heart! Stand any here that question God's judgment on a sinner? Behold! Behold a dreadful witness of it!"

With a convulsive motion, he tore away the ministerial band from before his breast. It was revealed! But it were irreverent to describe that revelation. For an instant, the gaze of the horror-stricken multitude was centered on the ghastly miracle; while the minister stood, with a flush of triumph in his face, as one who, in the crisis of acutest pain, had won a great victory. Then, down he sank upon the scaffold! Hester partly raised him, supporting his head against her bosom. Old Roger Chillingworth knelt down beside him, with a blank, dull countenance, out of which all life seemed to have departed.

"Thou hast escaped me! Thou hast escaped me!" he cried hoarsely.

[5] stigma: mark of infamy or disgrace

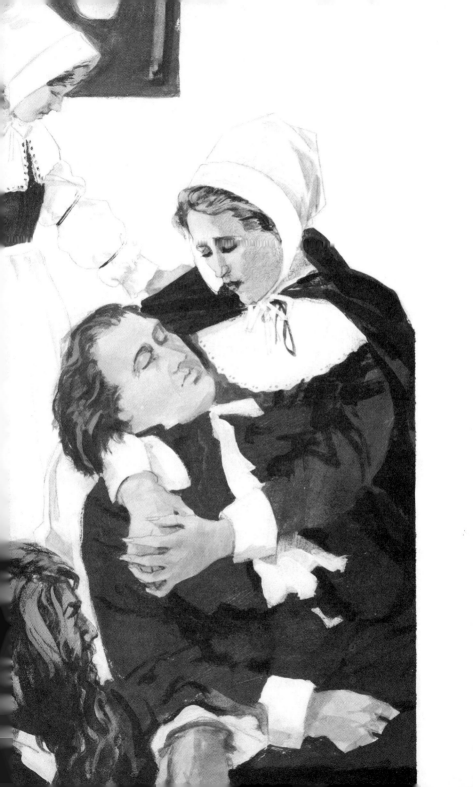

"May God forgive thee!" said the minister. "Thou, too, hast deeply sinned!"

He withdrew his dying eyes from the old man, and fixed them on the woman and the child.

"My little Pearl," said he feebly,—and there was a sweet and gentle smile over his face, as of a spirit sinking into deep repose; "dear little Pearl, wilt thou kiss me *now*? Thou wouldst not, yonder, in the forest! But *now* thou wilt?"

Pearl kissed his lips. A spell was broken. The great scene of grief in which the wild infant bore a part, had developed all her sympathies; and as her tears fell upon her father's cheek, they were the pledge that she would grow up amid human joy and sorrow, nor forever do battle with the world, but be a woman in it. Towards her mother, too, Pearl's errand as a messenger of anguish was all fulfilled.

"Hester," said the clergyman, "farewell!"

"Shall we not meet again?" whispered she, bending her face down close to him. "Shall we not spend our immortal life together? Surely, surely, we have paid the price for one another, with all this woe! Thou lookest far into eternity, with those bright dying eyes! Then tell me what thou seest?"

"Hush, Hester, hush!" said he. "The law we broke!— the sin here so awfully revealed!—let these alone be in thy thoughts! I fear! I fear! It may be that, when we forgot our God,—when we violated our reverence each for the other's soul,—it was thenceforth vain to hope that we could meet hereafter, in an everlasting and pure reunion. God knows; and He is merciful! He hath proved his mercy, most of all, in my afflictions. By giving me this burning torture to bear upon my breast! By sending yonder dark and terrible old man, to keep the torture always glowing at red-heat! By bringing me hither, to die this death of triumphant ignominy before the people! Had any of these agonies been wanting, I had been lost forever! Praised be His name! His will be done! Farewell!"

That final word came forth with the minister's last breath. The multitude, silent till then, broke out in a strange, deep voice of awe and wonder, which could not as yet find utterance, save in this murmur that rolled so heavily after the departed spirit.

24 *Pearl and Hester*

After some days, when time allowed the people to arrange their thoughts in reference to the foregoing scene, there were many accounts of what had been witnessed on the scaffold.

Most of the spectators testified to having seen, on the breast of the unhappy minister, a SCARLET LETTER—the very image of that worn by Hester Prynne—imprinted in the flesh. As regarded its origin, there were various explanation, all of which must necessarily have been of the nature of guesswork. Some declared that the Reverend Mr. Dimmesdale, on the very day when Hester Prynne first wore her ignominious badge, had begun a course of penance by inflicting a hideous torture on himself. Others claimed that the stigma had not been produced until long after, when old Roger Chillingworth, being a potent magician, had caused it to appear, through the agency of magic and poisonous drugs. Still others whispered their belief, that the awful symbol was the effect of the ever-active tooth of remorse, gnawing from the inmost heart outwardly, and at last manifesting Heaven's dreadful judgment by the visible presence of the letter. The reader may choose among these theories.

It is singular, nevertheless, that certain persons, who saw the whole scene, and professed never once to have

removed their eyes from the minister, denied that there
was any mark whatever on his breast, more than on a
newborn infant's. Neither, by their report, had his dying
words acknowledged, nor even remotely implied, any connection, on his part, with the guilt for which Hester Prynne
had so long worn the scarlet letter. According to these
highly respectable witnesses, the minister, conscious that
he was dying,—conscious, also, that the reverence of the
multitude placed him already among saints and angels,—
had desired, by yielding up his breath in the arms of that
fallen woman, to express to the world how utterly worthless
is the choicest of man's own righteousness. After exhausting his life in his efforts for mankind's spiritual good, he
had made the manner of his death a parable,[1] in order to
impress on his admirers the mighty and mournful lesson,
that, in the view of Infinite Purity, we are all sinners. It
was to teach them, that the holiest among us has but
attained so far above his fellows as to discern more clearly
the Mercy which looks down, and to repudiate more utterly
the phantom of human merit, which would look aspiringly
upward. Without disputing a truth so important, we must
be allowed to consider this version as only an instance of
that stubborn fidelity with which a man's friends—and
especially a clergyman's—will sometimes uphold his character, when proofs, clear as the mid-day sunshine on the
scarlet letter, make him a false and sin-stained creature of
the dust.

The authority which we have chiefly followed,—a
manuscript of old date, drawn up from the verbal testimony
of individuals, some of whom had known Hester Prynne,
while others had heard the tale from contemporary witnesses,—fully confirms the view taken in the foregoing
pages.

Nothing was more remarkable than the change which

[1] parable: a short story with a moral

took place, almost immediately after Dimmesdale's death, in the appearance and manner of the old man known as Roger Chillingworth. All his strength and energy—all his vital and intellectual force—seemed at once to desert him; insomuch that he positively withered up, shrivelled away, and almost vanished from mortal sight, like an uprooted weed that lies wilting in the sun. This unhappy man had made the very principle of his life the pursuit and systematic exercise of revenge; and when, by its completest triumph and consummation, that evil principle was left with no further material to support it, when, in short, there was no more Devil's work on earth for him to do, it only remained for the unhumanized mortal to betake himself whither his Master would find him tasks enough, and pay him his wages duly. But to all these shadowy beings, so long our close acquaintances,—as well Roger Chillingworth as his companions,—we would fain be merciful. It is a curious subject of observation and inquiry, whether hatred and love be not the same thing at bottom. Each, in its utmost development, supposes a high degree of intimacy and heart-knowledge; each makes one individual dependent for the food of his affections and spiritual life upon another; each leaves the passionate lover, or the passionate hater, desolate by the withdrawal of his subject.

Leaving this discussion apart, we have a matter of business to tell the reader. At old Roger Chillingworth's decease (which took place within the year), and by his last will and testament, of which Governor Bellingham and the Reverend Mr. Wilson were executors, he bequeathed a large amount of property, both here and in England, to little Pearl, the daughter of Hester Prynne and Arthur Dimmesdale.

So Pearl became the richest heiress of her day, in the New World. Not improbably, this circumstance wrought a very material change in public opinion; and, had the

mother and child remained here, little Pearl, at a marriage-
able age, might have mingled her wild blood with the
lineage of the devoutest Puritan among them all. But, soon
after the physician's death, the wearer of the scarlet letter
disappeared, and Pearl with her. For many years, though
a vague report would now and then find its way across the
sea, yet no definite tidings of them were received. The
story of the scarlet letter grew into a legend. Its spell,
however, was still potent, and kept the scaffold awful
where the poor minister had died, and likewise the cottage
by the seashore, where Hester Prynne had lived. Near this
latter spot, one afternoon, some children at play beheld a
tall woman, in a gray robe, approach the cottage-door. In
all those years it had never once been opened; but either
she unlocked it, or the decaying wood and iron yielded to
her hand, or she glided shadowlike through these obstacles,—at all events, she went in.

On the threshold she paused,—turned partly round,—
for, perchance the idea of entering all alone, and all so
changed, the home of so intense a former life, was more
dreary and desolate than even she could bear. But though
her hesitation was only for an instant, it was long enough
to display a scarlet letter on her breast.

Yes, it was Hester Prynne, who had returned, and
taken up her long-forsaken shame! But where was little
Pearl? If still alive she must now have been in the flush
and bloom of early womanhood. None knew—nor ever
learned, with perfect certainty—whether the elf-child had
gone thus untimely to her grave, or whether her wild, rich
nature had been softened and subdued, and made capable
of a woman's gentle happiness. But, through the remainder
of Hester's life, there were indications that she of the scarlet letter was the object of love and interest with some
inhabitant of another land. Letters came, with armorial[2]

2 armorial: pertaining to the coat of arms of a noble family

seals upon them, though of unknown design. In the cottage there were articles of comfort and luxury such as Hester never used, but which only wealth could have purchased, and affection have given. There were trifles, too, little ornaments, beautiful tokens of a continual remembrance, that must have been wrought by delicate fingers at the impulse of a fond heart. And, once, Hester was seen embroidering a baby-garment, with such a lavish richness of golden fancy as would have raised a public tumult, had any infant, thus apparelled, been shown to our sober-hued community.

In fine, the gossips of that day believed,—and Mr. Surveyor Pue, who made investigations a century later, believed,—and one of his recent successors in office, moreover, faithfully believes,—that Pearl was not only alive, but married, happy, and mindful of her mother, and that she would most joyfully have entertained that sad and lonely mother at her fireside.

But there was a more real life for Hester Prynne here, in New England, than in that unknown region where Pearl had found a home. *Here* had been her sin; *here,* her sorrow; and *here* was yet to be her penitence. She had returned, therefore, and resumed,—of her own free will, for not the sternest magistrate of that iron period would have imposed it,—resumed the symbol of which we have related so dark a tale. Never again did she remove it. But, in the lapse of the toilsome, thoughtful, and self-devoted years that made up Hester's life, the scarlet letter ceased to be a stigma which attracted the world's scorn and bitterness, and became a type of something to be sorrowed over, and looked upon with awe, yet with reverence too. And, as Hester Prynne had no selfish ends, nor lived for her own profit and enjoyment, people brought all their sorrows and perplexities, and besought her counsel, as one who had herself gone through a mighty trouble. Women, more especially,—

in the continually recurring trials of wounded, wasted, wronged, misplaced, or erring and sinful passion,—or with the dreary burden of a heart unyielded, because unvalued and unsought,—came to Hester's cottage, asking why they were so wretched, and what the remedy! Hester comforted and counselled them as best she might. She assured them, too, of her firm belief, that, at some brighter period, when the world should have grown ripe for it, in Heaven's own time a new truth would be revealed, in order to establish the whole relationship between man and woman on a surer ground of mutual happiness. Earlier in life, Hester had vainly imagined that she herself might be the destined prophetess, but had long since recognized the impossibility that any mission of divine and mysterious truth should be confided to a woman stained with sin, bowed down with shame, or even burdened with a life-long sorrow. The angel and apostle of the coming revelation must be a woman indeed, but one lofty, pure, and beautiful; and wise, moreover, not through dusky grief, but through joy; and showing how sacred love should make up happy, by the truest test of a life successful to such an end!

So said Hester Prynne, and glanced at the scarlet letter. And, after many, many years a new grave was dug near an old and sunken one, in that burial-ground beside which King's Chapel has since been built. It was near that old and sunken grave, yet with a space between, as if the dust of the two sleepers had no right to mingle. Yet one tombstone served for both. All around, there were monuments carved with armorial bearings; and on this simple slab of slate there appeared an engraved design. It bore a device, a herald's wording[3] of which might serve for a

---

[3] herald's wording: A herald is an officer who grants and records arms and lists the creation of earls. All questions relating to coats-of-arms are dealt with by the Heralds' College.

motto and brief description of our now concluded legend;
so sombre is it, and relieved only by one ever-glowing point
of light gloomier than the shadow:—

"ON A FIELD, BLACK, THE LETTER A, RED."

REVIEWING

YOUR

READING

CHAPTER 1

Finding the Main Idea
1. The purpose of this chapter is to
   a. introduce the main characters   **b.** set the scene and tone of the story   **c.** poke fun at the Puritans   **d.** tell what has happened before the story begins

Remembering Detail
2. Two things a new settlement must have are
   a. a courthouse and a post office   **b.** a village green and a church   **c.** a prison and a cemetery   **d.** a school and a hospital
3. The prison described is in
   a. an imaginary town   **b.** Boston   **c.** Salem   **d.** New York
4. Near the door of the prison grows
   a. a fig tree   **b.** poison ivy   **c.** a lilac bush   **d.** a rose bush
5. The street in front of the prison is made of
   a. dirt   **b.** cobblestones   **c.** gravel   **d.** blacktop

Appreciating Language
6. When he calls it *beetle-browed*, the author means that the prison
   a. resembles an insect   **b.** has an upper part that over-hangs the street   **c.** has gables   **d.** has round windows

THINKING IT OVER
The author says that even an ideal community needs a cemetery and a prison. What does this imply? Do you agree? Explain.

CHAPTER 2

Finding the Main Idea
1. The purpose of this chapter is to
   a. introduce Hester and show her punishment   **b.** show the cruelty of the townspeople   **c.** explain why Hester wears a scarlet letter   **d.** describe justice in Puritan New England

Remembering Detail
2. A large crowd has gathered because
   a. it is market day   **b.** a ship is expected from England   **c.** people want to witness Hester's punishment   **d.** it is a holiday
3. A device for punishment that is *not* mentioned in this chapter is the
   a. guillotine   **b.** rack   **c.** pillory   **d.** whipping post
4. Hester was born and grew up
   a. in an English village   **b.** in a European city
   c. in Boston   **d.** on a southern plantation
5. Part of Hester's punishment is to
   a. have her head and hands locked in the pillory
   b. be whipped   **c.** be branded   **d.** stand on the scaffold for a certain time

Drawing Conclusions
6. Most of the women of Boston consider Hester's punishment
   a. too harsh   **b.** fitting   **c.** shocking   **d.** not harsh enough

Appreciating Language
7. As used in the chapter, the word *gossips* seems to mean most nearly
   a. tattletales   **b.** friends   **c.** citizens   **d.** relatives

THINKING IT OVER
The women of the town show less pity for Hester than the men. What kind of crime do you think would be likely to arouse such anger in the women of Puritan Boston?

CHAPTER 3

Finding the Main Idea

1. The chapter is mostly about
   a. Hester's earlier life   **b.** the appearance of a mysterious stranger   **c.** justice in Puritan Boston   **d.** Hester's naming the father of her baby

Remembering Detail

2. The Indian who accompanies the stranger has been acting as his
   a. servant   **b.** slave   **c.** guide   **d.** captor
3. Until recently, the stranger has been
   a. a captive of Indians   **b.** in prison   **c.** the survivor of a shipwreck   **d.** a sea captain
4. Hester has been living in Boston
   a. all her life   **b.** about two years   **c.** three or four months   **d.** about ten years
5. Master Dimmesdale is
   a. a visiting clergyman   **b.** a doctor   **c.** the governor of Massachusetts   **d.** the pastor of a church in Boston

Identifying the Tone

6. Which of the following best describes Hester's reaction to seeing the stranger?
   a. joy   **b.** relief   **c.** indifference   **d.** distress

Appreciating Language

7. When the Governor tells Dimmesdale that it *behooves* him to urge Hester to repent, he means that it would be
   a. the wrong thing to do   **b.** the right thing to do   **c.** useless to do   **d.** the gentlemanly thing to do

Using Logic to Find Deeper Meaning

8. The stranger that Hester dreads being alone with is probably
   a. the father of her baby   **b.** her husband   **c.** her father   **d.** a messenger
9. Although the author does not say so, the A on Hester's dress must stand for
   a. adventuress   **b.** adulteress   **c.** author   **d.** angel

THINKING IT OVER

When Hester refuses to name the father of her baby, Dimmesdale wonders at the "wonderful strength and generosity of a woman's heart." In what way does he see her refusal as being generous? Explain.

CHAPTER 4

Finding the Main Idea

1. The chapter is mostly about
   a. Hester's repentance   b. Hester's meeting with Chillingworth   c. the baby's illness   d. life in prison

Remembering Detail

2. The length of time Chillingworth spent living with the Indians was
   a. about a year   b. about two years   c. a few weeks
   d. about a month
3. Chillingworth has learned about the healing properties of plants from
   a. books on alchemy   b. his years in medical school
   c. Indians   d. a former servant
4. Chillingworth asks Hester to
   a. come live with him   b. change her name   c. let him bring up the baby   d. keep his identity a secret
5. Chillingworth tells Hester that he is sure that
   a. they will be reunited someday   b. he knows who the baby's father is   c. she will not have to wear the scarlet letter forever   d. he will find out who the baby's father is

Drawing Conclusions

6. Chillingworth's Indian captors have released him
   a. out of pity   b. in hope of getting a ransom   c. in return for secrets of alchemy   d. at his wife's request

THINKING IT OVER

What reason does Chillingworth give Hester for his decision to remain in Boston? Does this reason make sense to you? Explain.

CHAPTER 5

Finding the Main Idea
1. The purpose of this chapter is to
   a. describe Hester's life after prison   b. describe the society life of Boston   c. show Hester's skill at needlework
   d. describe Chillingworth's revenge

Remembering Detail
2. Hester is never asked to make
   a. baby clothes   b. ceremonial costumes   c. wedding veils   d. clothing for the dead at funerals
3. Hester spends any extra money she has on
   a. fancy clothing for herself   b. helping Chillingworth
   c. helping the needy   d. furniture
4. The only ornament on Hester's own clothing is
   a. a simple pin   b. the scarlet letter   c. a locket
   d. a bit of lace
5. The poor people that Hester helps are
   a. grateful   b. sympathetic   c. friendly   d. ungrateful
6. Hester believes that the scarlet letter gives her the power to
   a. tell fortunes   b. recognize other sinners   c. cast spells   d. sew better

Identifying the Tone
7. Which of the following best describes the behavior of the people of Boston toward Hester?
   a. kindly   b. indifferent   c. heartless   d. tolerant

THINKING IT OVER
1. The author says that the art of needlework was "then, as now, almost the only one within a woman's grasp." Does this mean women had no other talents? Explain.
2. Explain why Hester's needlework was never called for on bridal costumes.

CHAPTER 6

Finding the Main Idea
1. In this chapter, the author is mostly interested in telling about
   a. Hester's social life   **b.** Pearl's nature   **c.** childhood in old Boston   **d.** Puritan family life

Remembering Detail
2. Hester called her child Pearl because
   a. that was her mother's name   **b.** of the child's pale complexion   **c.** the child was her only treasure   **d.** Chillingworth liked the name
3. In Puritan days, family discipline was
   a. lax   **b.** rigid   **c.** permissive   **d.** largely ignored
4. Pearl's nature is
   a. placid   **b.** timid   **c.** wild   **d.** gentle
5. Pearl's usual playmates are
   a. neighborhood children   **b.** poor children   **c.** imaginary creatures   **d.** old people
6. From infancy, Pearl has been fascinated by
   a. the sea   **b.** the forest   **c.** Indians   **d.** the scarlet letter

THINKING IT OVER
Much as she loves her daughter, Hester is deeply concerned about Pearl's wildness. Why is she more worried than most mothers would be about such a child? Explain.

CHAPTER 7

Remembering Detail

1. One reason for Hester's visiting the Governor's mansion is to

   a. seek a pardon **b.** deliver a pair of gloves **c.** seek advice about raising Pearl **d.** request more work

2. Some important people of Boston wish to

   a. take Pearl away from Hester **b.** drive Hester and Pearl out of town **c.** find a husband for Hester **d.** put Pearl in school

3. The red tunic that Hester made for Pearl resembles

   a. a clown's costume **b.** the scarlet letter **c.** a rainbow **d.** a sunset

4. The armor hanging in the Governor's hall

   a. is strictly for decoration **b.** belonged to an ancestor of the Governor's **c.** has actually been worn by the Governor **d.** dates back to Roman times

Drawing Conclusions

5. The scarlet letter looks huge reflected in the armor because

   a. the armor is so highly polished **b.** the curved surface distorts the image **c.** Pearl is so small **d.** the scarlet letter has grown bigger

THINKING IT OVER

What does the appearance of Governor Bellingham's house tell you about him as a person? Is it the kind of house you would expect an important Puritan to live in? Explain.

CHAPTER 8

Finding the Main Idea

1. The chapter is mostly about how
   a. Chillingworth has changed   b. Hester is able to keep Pearl   c. Hester is tempted by a witch   d. Pearl impresses the Governor with her piety
2. At this point, Pearl's age is about
   a. three   b. ten   c. six months   d. seven
3. When Master Wilson examines Pearl in religion, she
   a. impresses him with her knowledge   b. intentionally gives unsatisfactory answers   c. refuses to say a word   d. pretends she is a Quaker
4. The person to whom Hester appeals for help is
   a. Master Wilson   b. Governor Bellingham   c. Arthur Dimmesdale   d. Roger Chillingworth
5. The Black Man that Mistress Hibbins wants Hester to meet is really
   a. Chillingworth   b. Pearl's father   c. an Indian chief   d. the Devil

Drawing Conclusions

6. When Master Wilson says it would be sinful to pry further into the mystery of who Pearl's father is, Chillingworth is probably
   a. convinced   b. doubtful   c. wholly unconvinced   d. impressed

THINKING IT OVER

Hester tells Mistress Hibbins she would willingly go to meet the Black Man if the Governor had taken Pearl away from her. What does Hester mean by this? Do you think she means it seriously? Explain.

CHAPTER 9

Finding the Main Idea

1. This chapter is mostly about
   a. how Chillingworth learned to practice medicine
   b. how Chillingworth and Dimmesdale become closely associated   c. Dimmesdale's decision not to marry
   d. Chillingworth's anger at Hester

Remembering Detail

2. Before the arrival of Chillingworth, the only person practicing as a physician in Boston was
   a. Master Wilson   b. a druggist   c. Mistress Hibbins
   d. an Indian medicine man
3. Dimmesdale's health begins to decline
   a. after he meets Chillingworth   b. before Chillingworth comes to town   c. before Dimmesdale leaves England
   d. after he moves into the widow's house
4. Most of the people in Boston think that Chillingworth
   a. may be able to cure Dimmesdale   b. is an imposter
   c. is trying to kill Dimmesdale   d. is really Pearl's father
5. After settling in Boston, Chillingworth's appearance becomes
   a. more attractive   b. uglier   c. more spiritual
   d. more cheerful

Drawing Conclusions

6. Dimmesdale finally agrees to see the physician because
   a. he is feeling worse   b. he wants to get to know Chillingworth   c. members of his church urge him to do so
   d. he is terrified of dying

Appreciating Language

7. When Chillingworth says, "Good men ever interpret themselves too *meanly*," he means "too
   a. viciously"   b. humbly"   c. selfishly"   d. highly"

Using Logic to Find Deeper Meaning

8. The fact that Chillingworth is so readily accepted as a physician suggests that
a. his reputation as a healer has preceded him   **b.** medicine was primitive in those days   **c.** he has a strong influence with the Governor   **d.** he once attended medical school

THINKING IT OVER

Two contrasting views of Chillingworth and his relationship to Dimmesdale are held by the people of Boston. Describe both the favorable and unfavorable views in your own words. Tell which one fits the situation better.

CHAPTER 10

Finding the Main Idea
1. The chapter is mostly about
   a. how drugs are made from plants   b. the relationship of Chillingworth to his patient   c. Pearl's education in religion   d. Dimmesdale's burst of anger

Remembering Detail
2. The herbs that Dimmesdale asks Chillingworth about were picked
   a. in the forest   b. near the prison   c. beside the scaffold   d. in the graveyard
3. Dimmesdale and Chillingworth see Hester and Pearl walking
   a. in the marketplace   b. in the garden of the Governor's mansion   c. in the graveyard   d. along the beach
4. The person Pearl calls the "old Black Man" is
   a. Dimmesdale   b. Chillingworth   c. the Devil
   d. Master Wilson
5. In his discussion with the minister, Chillingworth argues that a guilty person should
   a. confess publicly   b. keep the crime hidden   c. work for the poor   d. pray for forgiveness

Identifying the Tone
6. Which of the following best describes Chillingworth's feelings at the end of the chapter?
   a. amazed and joyous   b. angry and resentful
   c. regretful   d. quiet and thoughtful

Appreciating Language
7. The word *leech* in the title of this and the preceding chapter is an old word meaning
   a. selfish person   b. physician   c. patient   d. impostor

THINKING IT OVER
Dimmesdale argues that a person might conceal a crime in order to be able to do good to others. Do you agree with this view? Explain.

CHAPTER 11

Finding the Main Idea

1. The purpose of this chapter is to
   a. describe the minister's growing fame   b. show how deeply the minister is suffering   c. show the minister's affection for Hester and Pearl   d. show the minister's growing dislike of Chillingworth

Remembering Detail

2. As Dimmesdale begins to dislike Chillingworth more and more, he
   a. avoids him   b. pokes fun at him   c. continues to see him regularly   d. attacks him publicly
3. When the minister confesses from the pulpit to being sinful, the congregation
   a. is shocked   b. blames Hester   c. thinks he is exaggerating   d. demands a new minister
4. Dimmesdale's congregation is sure that he will
   a. die young   b. quarrel with Chillingworth   c. become the next governor   d. confess to being Pearl's father
5. In a locked, secret closet, the minister keeps
   a. a pistol   b. a book of love poems   c. a whip
   d. a lock of Hester's hair

Appreciating Language

6. In the expression "the *very* truth," the old meaning of the word *very* is
   a. mostly   b. real   c. opposite of   d. bitter

Using Logic to Find Deeper Meaning

7. The probable reason that Hester and Pearl appear in the minister's nightly visions is that
   a. he sees them often   b. Hester is a sinful person
   c. Chillingworth is always talking about them   d. he is Pearl's father

THINKING IT OVER

Hawthorne says that Dimmesdale has "spoken the very truth, and transformed it into . . . falsehood." Explain what the author means by this.

CHAPTER 12

Finding the Main Idea

1. The purpose of this chapter is to
   a. describe Governor Winthrop's death   b. show the effect guilt has had on the minister   c. show Chillingworth's concern for the minister's health
   d. paint a picture of Boston at night

Remembering Detail

2. Leaving his house late at night, the minister
   a. visits Hester's cottage   b. goes to his church pulpit
   c. climbs up on the scaffold   d. visits Governor Bellingham

3. Hester and Pearl are up late because
   a. Hester has taken measurements for a funeral robe
   b. they have been to a play   c. Hester has visited the Black Man   d. they have been away on a trip

4. Pearl asks the minister to
   a. come home with them   b. stand with them on the scaffold at noon the next day   c. pick a rose for her
   d. be her friend

5. Dimmesdale leaves behind him on the scaffold
   a. his hat   b. his prayer book   c. his glove   d. his cane

6. Dimmesdale's guilt draws him to the scaffold where Hester stood because he
   a. shares her guilt   b. has always felt sorry for her
   c. expects a crowd to be there   d. knows he will meet Chillingworth there

Using Logic to Find Deeper Meaning

7. Pearl's asking Dimmesdale to stand on the scaffold at noon with her and her mother shows that she
   a. is mischievous   b. knows he is her father   c. likes being with him   d. wants to impress her friends

THINKING IT OVER

Was it a meteor or a big letter A that lit up the night sky? Consider the information that the author gives you on pages 116–119, as well as the sexton's words at the end of the chapter. Then form your own opinion.

CHAPTER 13

Finding the Main Idea
1. The purpose of this chapter is to show how
   a. people's opinions of Hester have changed
   b. ungrateful people can be c. Hester needs
   Dimmesdale's help
   d. Pearl's behavior worries her mother

Remembering Detail
2. At this time in the story, Pearl's age is about
   a. three b. four c. seven d. thirteen
3. Hester is always ready when
   a. money is to be made b. sick people need care
   c. decisions have to be made d. wealthy people need a
   servant
4. Many people now believe that the scarlet A stands for
   a. Action b. Able c. Age d. Adaptability
5. Anne Hutchinson was a
   a. woman punished for adultery b. Puritan leader
   c. famous artist d. religious leader

Drawing Conclusions
6. When the author refers to "the iron link of mutual
   crime" that binds Hester and Dimmesdale, he means
   a. their belief in God b. their illicit love affair c. their
   part of original sin d. their hatred of Chillingworth

Using Logic to Find Deeper Meaning
7. When Hester wonders "whether it were not better to
   send Pearl at once to heaven," she is considering
   a. letting a rich family adopt Pearl b. enrolling Pearl
   in a religious order c. killing Pearl d. praying for a
   miracle

THINKING IT OVER
Hester feels better able to cope with Roger Chillingworth now
than she did seven years earlier, when he visited her in prison.
Explain why, in your own words.

CHAPTER 14

Finding the Main Idea

1. This chapter is mostly about
   a. a conversation between Hester and Chillingworth
   b. Chillingworth's admiration for Hester   **c.** new friends
   Pearl has made   **d.** Dimmesdale's future

Remembering Detail

2. Hester meets Chillingworth
   a. on the scaffold   **b.** at a beach   **c.** in the graveyard
   d. in the forest

3. Hester is struck that her husband has come to look like a
   a. saint   **b.** much younger person   **c.** fiend   **d.** kindly
   old man

4. Hester tells Chillingworth that she will
   a. keep his secret if he forgives Dimmesdale   **b.** no
   longer keep his secret   **c.** tell the Governor he is not a
   physician   **d.** no longer wear the scarlet letter

5. Hester urges Chillingworth to
   a. leave Boston   **b.** release her from her promise
   c. expose Dimmesdale   **d.** grant Dimmesdale his pardon

Drawing Conclusions

6. Pearl's reflection in the pool seems to be urging her to
   a. go for a swim   **b.** build a sand castle   **c.** drown herself   **d.** go for a walk

Using Logic to Find Deeper Meaning

7. Hester believes the change in Chillingworth is partly her
   fault because
   a. of her promise to him   **b.** her unfaithfulness caused
   him to seek revenge   **c.** she refused to live with him
   d. her actions caused him public humiliation

THINKING IT OVER

One reaction of the audience watching the kind of drama called
tragedy is a sense of the waste of noble qualities possessed by
the characters. Think of this novel as a tragedy and tell in your
own words what waste of noble qualities is involved for Hester, Chillingworth, and Dimmesdale.

CHAPTER 15

Remembering Detail

1. Pearl stops throwing stones when
   a. she fears she has injured a bird   **b.** she finds a jellyfish   **c.** Hester calls to her   **d.** all the birds have flown away

2. The decoration Pearl makes out of seaweed is
   a. a wreath   **b.** the letter A   **c.** a veil   **d.** a sash

3. When Pearl asks the meaning of the scarlet letter, Hester
   a. tells her   **b.** locks her in the closet   **c.** cries   **d.** lies to her

Identifying the Tone

4. In this chapter, Hester feels all of the following toward Chillingworth except
   a. resentment   **b.** repulsion   **c.** affection   **d.** hatred

Using Logic to Find Deeper Meaning

5. Pearl's connecting the minister's habit of holding his hand over his heart with the scarlet letter is
   a. childish fancy   **b.** wrongheaded   **c.** amusing
   d. correct

THINKING IT OVER

The author says that "In all the seven bygone years, Hester Prynne had never before been false to the symbol on her bosom." Explain how she has been false to it in this chapter. Do you think she is justified in doing what she does?

CHAPTER 16

Remembering Detail

1. One reason that Hester does not visit the minister in his study is that
   a. she does not know where he lives **b.** she would not be welcome **c.** she fears Chillingworth's interference **d.** people would guess their secret

2. Hester chooses to meet the minister
   a. in the forest **b.** on the beach **c.** in the graveyard **d.** in the marketplace

3. While in the forest, Pearl begs to hear a story about
   a. Hansel and Gretel **b.** England **c.** Chillingworth **d.** the Black Man

4. Pearl has heard about the Black Man from
   a. Hester **b.** a woman at a house they visited the night before **c.** the minister **d.** Chillingworth

Identifying the Tone

5. Which of the following best describes Hester's feeling when she tells Pearl that she has met the Black Man once?
   a. boastful **b.** amused **c.** indifferent **d.** regretful

THINKING IT OVER

Hester tells Pearl that she has met the Black Man once and that the scarlet letter is his mark. Does she mean this literally—that she has met the Black Man in the forest? If not, what does she mean?

CHAPTER 17

Finding the Main Idea

1. The chapter is mainly about
   a. Hester's earlier affair **b.** Hester's first real conversation with Dimmesdale in many years **c.** Pearl's naughtiness **d.** plans for Dimmesdale's new career

Remembering Detail

2. The time since Hester and Dimmesdale were lovers has been
   a. two years **b.** seven years **c.** six months **d** twenty years

3. The first things that Hester and the minister say to each other are
   a. small talk **b.** accusations **c.** warnings **d.** expressions of love

4. During the conversation between Hester and Dimmesdale, Pearl is
   a. secretly listening **b.** off playing **c.** sitting on the minister's lap **d.** home at the cottage

5. Hester reveals
   a. the identity of Pearl's father **b.** who Chillingworth really is **c.** her love for Dimmesdale **d.** her desire to leave Boston

Drawing Conclusions

6. In relation to themselves, Hester and Dimmesdale consider Chillingworth
   a. an injured person **b.** a misunderstanding friend
   c. a great sinner **d.** someone to confide in

7. The real reason that Dimmesdale does not leave Boston as Hester suggests is that
   a. he fears Chillingworth **b.** he doesn't want to leave her **c.** he lacks the strength to start a new life alone
   d. he doesn't want to leave his parishioners

THINKING IT OVER

At the end of the chapter, Hester assures Dimmesdale he will not have to venture into the world *alone*. What is she telling him? Is she revealing a plan that she made before meeting him? What do you think?

CHAPTER 18

Finding the Main Idea

1. The purpose of this chapter is to
   a. show how Hester has changed **b.** reveal Dimmesdale's decision to leave with Hester **c.** show Pearl's feelings toward Dimmesdale **d.** tell what Pearl has been doing in the forest

Remembering Detail

2. After removing the scarlet letter, Hester
   a. stamps it underfoot **b.** throws it beside the brook **c.** packs it carefully in her basket **d.** lets Pearl play with it
3. Once she has taken the scarlet letter off, Hester feels
   a. guilty **b.** relieved **c.** confused **d.** uneasy
4. Dimmesdale fears that Pearl
   a. will not recognize him **b.** will be afraid of him **c.** will not love him **d.** prefers Chillingworth to him
5. The one forest creature that Pearl does *not* meet is a
   a. partridge **b.** fox **c.** rabbit **d.** pigeon

THINKING IT OVER

In several places in this chapter, the forest is used as a symbol. What does it represent? Does it seem good, bad, or not clearly either one?

CHAPTER 19

Finding the Main Idea
1. This chapter is mostly about
   a. plans for the future   b. Pearl's reaction   c. Pearl's sense of humor   d. the minister's guilt

Remembering Detail
2. Dimmesdale confesses that he has feared that
   a. Pearl would die   b. Pearl would never know her father   c. Pearl would resemble him too much   d. Pearl was really Chillingworth's child
3. Dimmesdale tells Hester that children
   a. always like him   b. do not take to him   c. make him irritable   d. make him happy
4. On her return, Pearl is upset because
   a. Hester has removed the scarlet letter   b. she cannot play longer   c. the minister has spoken crossly to her
   d. she mistakes the minister for the Black Man
5. Pearl refuses to cross the brook until
   a. Dimmesdale carries her   b. Hester puts the scarlet letter back on   c. Hester threatens her with punishment
   d. Dimmesdale promises to walk into town with them

Identifying the Tone
6. Which of the following best describes Dimmesdale's feelings as he watches Pearl's slow return?
   a. joyous anticipation   b. curiosity   c. nervous anticipation   d. impatience

THINKING IT OVER
This chapter has been described as one of the most painful in the novel. What incidents make it so?

CHAPTER 20

Finding the Main Idea
1. This chapter is mostly about
   a. the minister's meeting with Chillingworth   **b.** the minister's meeting with Mistress Hibbins   **c.** how much the minister has changed   **d.** the minister's future plans

Remembering Detail
2. Hester and Dimmesdale plan to start a new life in
   a. New York   **b.** Boston   **c.** Europe   **d.** the forest
3. In three days, the minister plans to
   a. have revenge on Chillingworth   **b.** preach an important sermon   **c.** see another physician   **d.** marry Hester
4. The first person the minister meets on returning to town is
   a. Mistress Hibbins   **b.** a young girl from his congregation   **c.** Chillingworth   **d.** an elderly deacon
5. The language of the minister's Bible is
   a. English   **b.** Hebrew   **c.** Greek   **d.** Latin

Drawing Conclusions
6. When Mistress Hibbins refers to "yonder sovereign you know of," she means
   a. Apostle Eliot   **b.** Chillingworth   **c.** Charles the First   **d.** the Devil

Using Logic to Find Deeper Meaning
7. When Dimmesdale tells Chillingworth he expects to leave soon for "another world," he means
   a. heaven   **b.** hell   **c.** Europe   **d.** the forest

THINKING IT OVER
Discuss the ways in which Dimmesdale has changed since his meeting with Hester. Consider physical changes, changes in his outlook on life, and changes in his treatment of people he meets.

CHAPTER 21

Finding the Main Idea
1. This chapter is mostly about
   a. a public holiday   b. Hester's dreams of the future
   c. Pearl's behavior   d. the rowdiness of the sailors

Remembering Detail
2. The crowd has gathered to see a procession of
   a. Indian captives   b. captured pirates   c. the Governor
   and other dignitaries   d. jugglers and clowns
3. Men from the forest settlements wear
   a. coarse gray cloth   b. deerskin clothing   c. embroidered coats   d. black cloaks and pointed hats
4. The ship that is in port will sail for
   a. the Spanish Main   b. Bristol   c. New York
   d. Plymouth

Drawing Conclusions
5. These jolly sailors have not long before
   a. attempted a mutiny   b. committed acts of piracy
   c. battled with the Indians   d. lived respectable lives in England
6. An ordinary citizen who smoked tobacco in public would be
   a. preached against on Sunday   b. put in the stocks
   c. fined a shilling   d. made to stand on the scaffold

Using Logic to Find Deeper Meaning
7. The news Hester learns from the ship's captain tells her that
   a. Dimmesdale has changed his mind   b. Chillingworth has guessed the plans she and the minister have made
   c. Chillingworth wants her to live with him again
   d. Chillingworth has forgiven Dimmesdale

THINKING IT OVER
How do you suppose Chillingworth is able to guess the plan that Hester and the minister have formed? Did he have any warning that Hester and Dimmesdale would meet? Can he guess where they met? What might the minister's behavior tell him?

CHAPTER 22

Remembering Detail

1. In the procession, Dimmesdale seems unusually
   a. sad **b.** feeble **c.** energetic **d.** ill at ease
2. In Puritan days, a minister was
   a. taken for granted **b.** highly respected **c.** less
   honored than a politician **d.** a rare sight
3. Mistress Hibbins tells Hester that she knows
   a. Hester and the minister met in the forest **b.** Hester
   and the minister plan to run away **c.** Chillingworth is
   Hester's husband **d.** why Dimmesdale holds his hand
   over his heart
4. During Dimmesdale's sermon, Hester
   a. walks in the marketplace with Pearl **b.** stands in the
   back of the church **c.** remains near the scaffold
   d. walks in the graveyard
5. The shipmaster gives Pearl
   a. a kiss **b.** a silk scarf **c.** a pearl necklace **d.** a gold
   chain

Drawing Conclusions

6. The Indians in the crowd staring at Hester
   a. plan to kidnap her **b.** know the meaning of the scarlet letter **c.** misunderstand the meaning of the scarlet
   letter **d.** sympathize with Hester

THINKING IT OVER

The last sentence of the chapter suggests that both Dimmesdale
and Hester share "the same scorching brand of shame." What
do you think this means?

CHAPTER 23

Finding the Main Idea

1. This chapter is mostly about
   a. the revelation of Dimmesdale's secret   b. Chillingworth's disappointment   c. the reaction to the minister's sermon   d. the procession from the church

Remembering Detail

2. From the church, the procession was to move to
   a. Governor Bellingham's house   b. the prison
   c. the town hall   d. the ship
3. The audience shouts at the appearance of
   a. John Wilson   b. Governor Bellingham   c. an angel
   d. the minister
4. Dimmesdale stops as he reaches the
   a. church steps   b. town hall   c. prison   d. scaffold
5. The only person who tries to prevent Dimmesdale from mounting the scaffold is
   a. Governor Bellingham   b. Hester   c. Chillingworth
   d. John Wilson

Drawing Conclusions

6. Chillingworth tries to stop the minister from confessing because he
   a. pities him   b. doesn't want his revenge to end
   c. fears his own identity will be revealed   d. doesn't want Hester to be hurt more

Using Logic to Find Deeper Meaning

7. What the minister reveals on the scaffold is
   a. whip marks   b. a cross on his chest   c. a scarlet letter on his chest   d. a wound in his chest

THINKING IT OVER

Think about Dimmesdale's last words to Hester, Pearl, and Chillingworth. What feelings toward each does he express as he is dying?

CHAPTER 24

Finding the Main Idea

1. The purpose of this chapter is to
   a. prepare readers for a sequel   **b.** describe Hester's death scene   **c.** describe Chillingworth's repentance   **d.** round out the story

Remembering Detail

2. After the minister's death, Roger Chillingworth lives
   a. only a few days   **b.** many years   **c.** less than a year   **d.** seven years
3. Chillingworth leaves property to
   a. the church   **b.** Pearl   **c.** Hester   **d.** Mistress Hibbins
4. After Hester returns to Boston, she always wears
   a. colorful clothes   **b.** the scarlet letter as before   **c.** Pearl's gold chain   **d.** a locket containing Dimmesdale's portrait

Drawing Conclusions

5. By mentioning letters and gifts to Hester, the author suggests that
   a. Pearl is alive and happily married   **b.** Hester has an unknown admirer   **c.** the townspeople want to make up for their cruelty to her   **d.** Chillingworth is not dead after all

Using Logic to Find Deeper Meaning

6. Hester's grave is dug near that of
   a. Chillingworth   **b.** Pearl   **c.** Mistress Hibbins   **d.** Dimmesdale

THINKING IT OVER

Is the ending of the story satisfactory to you? Could the story have ended in any other way?